Walking with Biblical Women of Courage

The Bible Reading Fellowship
15 The Chambers, Vineyard
Abingdon OX14 3FE
brf.org.uk

The Bible Reading Fellowship (BRF) is a Registered Charity (233280)

ISBN 978 0 85746 533 7
First published 2017
10 9 8 7 6 5 4 3 2 1 0
All rights reserved

Text © Fiona Stratta 2017
The author asserts the moral right to be identified as the author of this work
Cover image © Thinkstock

Acknowledgements
Unless otherwise stated, scripture quotations taken from the Holy Bible, New Living Translation, copyright © 1996, 2004, 2007, 2013. Used by permission of Tyndale House Publishers, Inc., Carol Stream, Illinois 60188. All rights reserved.

Scripture quotations taken from The Holy Bible, New International Version (Anglicised edition) copyright © 1979, 1984, 2011 by Biblica. Used by permission of Hodder & Stoughton Publishers, a Hachette UK company. All rights reserved. 'NIV' is a registered trademark of Biblica. UK trademark number 1448790.

Scripture quotations taken from the Holy Bible, English Standard Version, published by HarperCollins Publishers, © 2001 Crossway Bibles, a division of Good News Publishers. Used by permission. All rights reserved.

Scripture taken from THE MESSAGE. Copyright © 1993, 1994, 1995, 1996, 2000, 2001, 2002. Used by permission of NavPress Publishing Group.

Every effort has been made to trace and contact copyright owners for material used in this resource. We apologise for any inadvertent omissions or errors, and would ask those concerned to contact us so that full acknowledgement can be made in the future.

A catalogue record for this book is available from the British Library

Printed and bound by CPI Group (UK) Ltd, Croydon CR0 4YY

Walking with
Biblical Women
of Courage

IMAGINATIVE STUDIES FOR BIBLE MEDITATION

FIONA STRATTA

Contents

Introduction

The following reflective monologues and studies are based on biblical accounts of women in the Old and New Testaments, and are intended for groups who meet together to grow in their relationships with God and each other, or for individual use. First the Bible passage about the woman to be studied is read by the group. Then they read the reflective monologue which is written as if the woman herself is speaking.

There are several types of Christian meditation; one of them is to 'enter' the scripture using the imagination. Imaginative reflection on the Bible is not a new concept; it was practiced by St Ignatius of Loyola in the 16th century. It can be a powerful way for God to speak to us, for imaginative meditation involves not only the mind, but also the emotions.

Superficially, we may feel very different to these women who lived so long ago but, as we hear their stories, we discover that we share much in common: joy and heartache; love and jealousy; difficult choices; the need for patience, wisdom and courage. Courage is a quality we all need and it comes in many different forms: courage to endure and adapt; courage to live under threat; courage to face a difficult future; courage to speak or stand out; courage to follow our convictions; courage to take on a challenging role; courage to sacrifice self for the sake of others. We read in 1 Corinthians 16:13–14, 'Be on guard. Stand firm in the faith. Be courageous. Be strong. And do everything with love.' As we prayerfully reflect on the lives of these lesser-known biblical women, a transformative work of the Holy Spirit takes place within, enabling us to become more courageous, more loving, more Christlike. We see God's wonderful grace, his undeserved favour and blessing, touching the lives of these women, and discover that this same grace is available to us.

Although the monologues follow the biblical accounts, not every detail will be true. After all, we are imagining, filling in the gaps with the possible. This need not be a problem, for it is precisely what we do when we tell Bible stories to children; we embellish the story to capture the child's imagination with the purpose of teaching the child spiritual truths. This is exactly what we are doing here.

Points for reflection and discussion follow the monologues, enabling issues to be explored and spiritual growth to take place. All questions may be considered or just a few, depending on the time available and the requirements of the group or individual. We discover the truth of Paul's words to Timothy: 'All scripture is inspired by God and is useful to teach us what is true and to make us realise what is wrong in our lives… God uses it to prepare and equip his people to do every good work' (2 Timothy 3:16–17). Sometimes verses are suggested for meditation: this involves a slow, deliberate and prayerful consideration of the verses, plumbing their depths. Like imaginative contemplation, it allows scripture to work in us. We grow in our relationship with God as Father, Son and Holy Spirit.

Finally, there is the opportunity to record what God has been saying to us and the implications for our individual spiritual journeys. After all, in coming to God's word, we want not only to learn, but also to change and to grow, so that we are not just 'hearers' of the word but 'doers'.

The monologues can be used in groups without the discussion element as a means of initiating a time of silent reflection or led meditation. They can also stand alone effectively in many other contexts; for example, individuals can use them in private meditation, or the monologues can be read to larger groups, such as congregations.

The facilitator

You will need to ensure that there are pens and paper and a variety of translations and paraphrases of the Bible.

It will be your responsibility to introduce the study and to find someone to read the reflective monologue. Try to ask someone gifted in reading aloud.

It is advisable to read through the discussion questions, including the Bible references, before your group meets. This will help you to facilitate the discussion better. Ensure you also allow enough time for personal reflection at the end. It may be helpful to play quiet music while individuals are completing their personal reflection.

Hagar (Part 1)

Introduction

- Read Genesis 16:1–15.

- Ask God to speak to you through this episode. You could use the words from Revelation 1:4: 'Grace and peace to you from the one who is, who always was, and who is still to come.'

- Sit back, relax and close your eyes. Imagine the scene as someone reads the monologue.

Monologue

While I fed him, he was mine, this child, this beautiful boy. Oh, I know Sarai saw him as her and Abram's son, but it was *me* who suckled him. It was *my* eyes he gazed into as he drank; it was *me* who dressed him, bathed him, sang songs to him and whispered lovingly in his ears. I discovered in him a joy and peace that I had never known before. As I looked out over all the wealth Abram had accumulated, I would tell my son that one day it would all be his.

In those early days, I was his world and he was mine.

The day that Sarai had given me to Abram, I had heard them in deep conversation, distress in Abram's voice, then insistence in Sarai's... and then silence, a long silence. Eventually, Sarai had stood before me, with Abram behind her, and given her instruction: 'You are to sleep with Abram, he needs an heir. You are to have the child on my behalf.'

As a servant it is better not to think, not to feel, not to hope, not to dream, to expect nothing in return for your labour, save food in your mouth and a place to sleep. Obey orders—that is what a servant must focus on doing; I had to obey Sarai's order. But this command transformed everything between us. A few months later, I knew for certain that I was pregnant. I felt needed, important. Servant that I was, my status altered from that moment. Who could look down on the woman carrying Abram's heir?

I changed—gone was the subservience; I was proud. I was giving Abram what *she* could not give him; for once, I had something that Sarai did not have, could not have—a child growing within me. I despised her and she knew it; even my sickness and tiredness taunted her. As my belly swelled, so did my pride. Who was she to order me around? The animosity between us grew; I sneered at her and she responded by weighing me down with increasing demands, until I could bear it no longer—I would go and my baby with me.

So I left at first light, taking the road to Shur. It was foolishness, I realise that now, but I wanted to break out from their control and make a life for myself and my child. Of course, I did not have the means. When the day was at its hottest, I sat down to rest by a spring of water in that vast wilderness; it was the well between Kadesh and Bered. The hopelessness of my situation became clear to me: what had seemed like freedom just twelve hours ago was in reality a different type of captivity, one without resources.

A voice broke through into my distressed thoughts, a voice that was to change the course of my life, a voice I would long to hear every day that I lived, such was its beauty: 'Hagar, Sarai's servant, where have you come from and where are you going?'

Who knew my name? I raised my head and, turning towards the source of the words, saw the figure of a man, although I instinctively knew that he was far more than a man. Before me was a being who filled me with both awe and peace simultaneously.

'I am running away from my mistress, Sarai,' I replied.

'Hagar, return and do all you can to live at peace with Sarai, be subject to her. I will look after you and the child.'

Who knew my circumstances? Who saw everything about me?

'*I*...' the being had promised, '*I* will look after you.' No other than the angel of the Lord, the God of Abram and Sarai, was speaking to *me*, a maidservant.

'I will give you more descendants than could possibly be counted. You are to call the son who will be born to you Ishmael—"the Lord has heard"; he has seen your misery.' Words of hope and comfort flowed from the angel of the Lord.

My child who, twelve hours ago, had been guaranteed a secure and wealthy future, kicked me from within. Was I to take that away from him to meet my own desire for independence? Yet *I* had needs: to be treated with consideration; to be valued. Now the Lord himself had promised to care for me.

'Your son will be strong and a wild donkey of a man. He will live in conflict with those around him and in hostility with his relatives.'

How his words made me tremble!

Suddenly I was quite alone, hearing only the murmuring spring and feeling nothing but the intense heat. I had to choose—his will or my will, his ways or my ways, my well-being or that of my child. God's voice was not one to ignore: that day the God of my mistress became my God. I had my own name for him: 'the One who sees me'.

Reflection and discussion

- Did any words or phrases stand out for you?

- Hagar, as Sarai's maidservant, had few choices in life. There are still many people without opportunity, trapped by their circumstances. Slavery exists in many forms around our world, and often much nearer at hand than we realise. Who comes to mind? How could you make a difference, individually, as a group or as a church?

- In the monologue, Hagar gains a sense of identity and purpose through bearing and nurturing Ishmael. Identity and purpose contribute greatly to our well-being and can come from many different areas of our lives. What gives you identity and purpose? A loss of identity and/or purpose can strike us at different times in life, perhaps causing stress and requiring adaptation. Share such times and how you moved through them. You may currently have lost your identity and/or purpose; if you feel able, ask others for prayer.

- Christ promises us identity and purpose in him. Meditate on the words in 2 Corinthians 5:17: 'Anyone who belongs to Christ has become a new person. The old life is gone; a new life has begun.' Are you at a stage of transition where you need to ask God what he wants to do in and through you next in your life?

- Hagar succumbs to the temptation to run away in order to escape her problems. Running away is often only a temporary solution and may bring its own problems, as we see so clearly in this episode. Are there times when you have been tempted to try to escape a challenging situation? If you are able, share these. Pray for the courage to face your trials with the Holy Spirit's help. Read and draw strength from Romans 5:3–5.

- Hagar found herself in a new captivity: lack of resources. Many throughout our world and in our own communities are trapped by poverty, even homelessness. Others leave their homes in the hope of building a better life and find themselves living in hard and life-threatening conditions. Spend some time praying for these people and for those who seek both to relieve their suffering and to help them build a better future.

- Hagar is described as being filled with 'awe and peace simultaneously'. Are there occasions when you have experienced very different, even conflicting, emotions at the same time? Share them. Paul writes, 'Our hearts ache, but we always have joy. We are poor, but we give spiritual riches to others. We own nothing, and yet we have everything' (2 Corinthians 6:10). What do you understand from this verse?

- The angel of the Lord asks Hagar, 'Where have you come from and where are you going?' God obviously knew the answers to these questions, so what was Hagar being asked to ponder on a deeper level? The God who wants us to consider our past and ask for forgiveness also offers us hope for the future. How would you answer God if he asked you these questions?

- In the monologue we see Hagar's struggles between doing what is best for her unborn child and meeting her own needs, 'to be treated with consideration; to be valued'. We may face similar conflicts between meeting the needs of those entrusted to us and satisfying our own human need to be cared for and valued. How can we get the balance? Share your experiences.

- It must have taken Hagar courage to return and face the future. Her encounter with 'the One who sees me' (Genesis 16:13, NIV) enabled her to do this. God sees all that happens to us and is active in giving us wisdom, as he did to Hagar: 'If you need wisdom, ask our generous God, and he will give it to you' (James 1:5). How have you experienced the 'God of seeing' (Genesis 16:13,

ESV)? Are there situations you are facing where you need courage? If you are able, share these and pray for one another.

Conclusion

Take time to pray through your findings. What might God be saying to you? Is anything particularly relevant to your life at the moment? Write down what you have learnt and refer back to it regularly in the days ahead so that it becomes part of your thinking, reacting and lifestyle.

Hagar (Part 2)

Introduction

- Read Genesis 21:1–20.

- Ask God to speak to you through this episode. You could use the words from 2 Peter 3:18: 'But grow in the grace and knowledge of our Lord and Saviour Jesus Christ. To him be glory both now and for ever! Amen' (NIV).

- Sit back, relax and close your eyes. Imagine the scene as someone reads the monologue.

Monologue

I said nothing on my return and they said nothing to me. I saw relief on Abram's face; perhaps even a little relief crossed Sarai's tense brow. From that time on, I showed her respect, quietly following her wishes and scarcely looking her in the eyes.

So much was mine—the pain and joy of the birth, the delight of nursing Ishmael and the bond between us. There were so many moments of pure delight for me as I watched Ishmael grow up in the position of future heir, enjoying its privileges and pleasures. Life seemed very settled, that is, until Abram, on God's instruction, ordered that all the males should be circumcised. Apparently it was the way for Abram (or Abraham, as he insisted God now wanted him to be called) to set apart all that God had given him, ready for God to fulfil his promise— the provision of many descendants, more numerous than the grains of sand.[1] These offspring, I knew, would come through Ishmael.

Abraham seemed troubled after this encounter with God and I noticed that his attitude towards me, Ishmael and Sarah (as he now called his wife) had subtly changed.

Not long after that three visitors arrived. I recognised one of them as no one other than the angel of the Lord. They told Sarah that she would have a child within the year. I laughed to myself; she was too old, it was impossible... wasn't it?[2] But six months later there was no denying it: my mistress was very clearly with child. The joy when her baby, Isaac (meaning laughter), was born resounded throughout the tent. I silently carried on following orders, helping to care for this child, believing that it was my Ishmael who was the heir, trusting Abraham that Ishmael's future was secure. I continued to prepare him for his role at every opportunity, but something in my boy altered. He saw Abraham's pleasure in Isaac and gradually his envy turned to outright jealousy. Ishmael's place at the heart of the family had been usurped.

Abraham arranged a celebration to mark Isaac being weaned. While serving, I noticed Isaac and Ishmael together; it seemed harmless play, but then I noticed a glint in Ishmael's eyes. There was a pained and surprised expression on Isaac's face. I saw that Sarah had seen the incident too. As I cleared away I heard angry words between Sarah and Abraham. Was Ishmael to be punished, I wondered?

Punished—if only it had been that simple. I saw Abraham walk away and Sarah busied herself with Isaac, ignoring me except for the occasional instruction. Ishmael kept his distance. We both saw Abraham return and speak to Sarah—his head bent low with resignation and hers raised in triumph. So what was the punishment to be? Nothing was said, though, for the rest of the day. I tossed and turned that night in my anxiety, only to be woken early by Abraham.

'Get up and get Ishmael,' he commanded.

I did as any servant does—I obeyed. Once we were up, Abraham placed a bag of food and a container of water on my back. Surely not—before I had run away, but this time was I to be sent away? Surely not...

'But Ishmael,' I cried. 'Your son!'

'My heir will be Isaac. God will make a great nation through him. God has told me so.'

The words were a knife to my heart, but I obeyed, as servants do. Abraham walked with us a while, then he embraced Ishmael and at that moment they both looked shattered. 'What sort of God is it that asks you to abandon your son?' I wanted to shout at Abraham. 'What sort of man are you who obeys God even when your heart is breaking?'

As we walked aimlessly on and on, our shock and anger receded, as did our supplies, until all that was left was our despair and exhaustion. Ishmael collapsed before me, for at that age he was growing fast and his energies faded quickly without constant food. I held him as long as I could, sitting under the shade of a bush, watching him slip into unconsciousness. There is no greater pain for a mother than to be unable to save her child from death. I could not bear it. Sure that he was no longer aware of my presence, I stumbled away. I could not watch him die. I fell to the ground and wept.

'God, where are you? What of your promises to care for us?'

Then, in the silence, I heard the voice that breathes peace.

'Look up, Hagar, do not be afraid. Comfort the child. I will look after you and Ishmael. He will father a great nation; the promises will be fulfilled.'

I looked up and, so near at hand, was a well. How had I not noticed it? It was full of water and, quickly refilling our container, I took some to Ishmael, poured some over his burning forehead, over his parched lips and slowly he started to revive and drink.

'We will live,' I whispered. 'God is faithful.'

Footnote

Hagar brought Ishmael up in the wilderness of Paran. Later she arranged for him to marry an Egyptian. He was indeed wild and strong and became a skilled archer. Ishmael had twelve sons (1 Chronicles 1:29–31) and their descendants became known as the Ishmaelites.

Reflection and discussion

- Did any words or phrases stand out for you?

- In many ways, Hagar's attitude to Sarai was justified and yet, as we saw at the end of the last monologue, God instructed her to go back and submit to Sarai's authority, which she does. Are there situations in which you have struggled or are struggling to demonstrate submission? Sometimes it can take more courage to submit than to fight. Can you think of examples?

- Circumcision was part of the covenant in which Abraham set all that he was and all that he had apart for God. We are instructed to circumcise our hearts in Deuteronomy 30:6. What do you think this means in practice?

- Hagar had to live in difficult circumstances as the result of others' choices. Has this ever happened to you? If you feel able, share this with others. We cannot choose all our circumstances but we can choose our reactions, as Hagar does in the monologue when she returns to Sarai and behaves with humility. Sometimes a change in attitude and reactions can alter a situation or relationship for the better. Working on our attitudes can take courage, but has the benefit of developing resilience within us. Encourage each other by sharing experiences of this. Read and perhaps learn by heart Philippians 4:8.

- In her agony Hagar thinks, 'What sort of God is it that asks you to abandon your son?' and 'What sort of man are you who obeys God even when your heart is breaking?' It is the same God who was prepared to abandon his only Son to death on a cross for our salvation (Matthew 27:46); the Christ who was prepared to obey God even when his heart was breaking (Luke 22:41–44); the Lord whom we can call out to with total honesty (Psalm 22:1–2); the one who has carried our griefs and sorrows. Take time this week to meditate on Isaiah 53.

- Hagar's circumstances are the result of Sarah having made her own plans rather than waiting for God's timing. Yet God's provision goes far beyond Sarah's errors: God has a plan for Ishmael too. In a mysterious way, it can be hard for us to understand that God's plan incorporates our mistakes. If you feel able, share your experiences of this.

- Hagar was in a desperate situation when God's provision came to her. We can sometimes be at the end of our tether when a prayer is finally answered. Read Isaiah 58:11. How has hanging on to promises such as these helped you in difficult times? Are there Bible promises that have sustained you? How have you experienced God in and through your difficulties?

Conclusion

Take time to pray through your findings. What might God be saying to you? Is anything particularly relevant to your life at the moment? Write down what you have learnt and refer back to it regularly in the days ahead so that it becomes part of your thinking, reacting and lifestyle.

Shiphrah, Puah and Jochebed

Introduction

- Read Exodus 1:1—2:10 and Numbers 26:59.

- Ask God to speak to you through this episode. You could praise God for the commands and promises in Deuteronomy 31:6: 'So be strong and courageous!... For the Lord your God will personally go ahead of you. He will neither fail you nor abandon you.'

- Sit back, relax and close your eyes. Imagine the scene as three people read the monologues.

Monologues

Puah

'When you help the Hebrew women in childbirth and observe them on the delivery stool, if it is a boy, kill him, if it is a girl, let her live.'[1] Pharaoh's command came as a terrible shock to us. How could we do this? Our role was to aid these women, to do all in our power, knowledge and skill to hand them live, healthy babies. Shiphrah and I had worked together for many years, supporting the Hebrew women on the birthing stools, easing their babies into daylight. We could not count how many times we had known the joy of a safe delivery. There had been terrible times, too, when the baby was stillborn, or born too early to survive; then we had shared the mother's grief. More terrible yet had been the occasions when we could not save the mother's life. Oh yes, we knew the agony of death associated with childbirth. How could we fulfil this command? It went against everything we stood for, everything we believed in. Our God, the God of the Hebrews, we knew from our history, would be against such cruelty.

Shiphrah

We remembered God's promise to Abraham—how a great nation would arise from his offspring. His son, Isaac, had married Rebecca who gave birth to twins, Esau and Jacob. Jacob had twelve sons, and one of these, Judah, had also fathered twins, Zerah and Perez, born to Tamar. What a hard birth that had been for Tamar and what a difficult delivery for the midwife.[2] Two boys saved at birth and later kept alive during famine by their family's move to Egypt. There, Jacob's sons were fruitful: delivery after delivery,[3] baby boys and girls who grew to become strong men and women. For years, the Israelites knew such great blessing, until the Egyptian king became afraid of these numerous, robust men whom he feared might turn against him.

First Pharaoh attempted to subdue our people by force, stealing our freedom by making us slaves. The relationship between Egyptian and Israelite turned to one of hatred—a hatred springing from fear, unleashing the worst in human nature. Egypt's wealth, with its beautiful cities in the Nile delta, was created by the enslaved bodies of young Hebrew men and their fathers. With God's sustenance, the Hebrews survived, reaching their taskmasters' harsh targets. As the slave drivers' fear of these tremendously strong Hebrew men escalated, so their demands grew. Our men now had to make the bricks themselves and spent all their waking hours building, or tending the Egyptians' fields. It is no surprise that their hostility grew. Their sons were raised in bitterness, believing that life had no more to offer them than slavery. Yet some hung on to the words, 'But I will punish the nation they serve as slaves, and afterwards they will come out with great possessions.'[4]

Puah

'When you help the Hebrew women in childbirth and observe them on the delivery stool, if it is a boy, kill him, if it is a girl, let her live.'[5] Pharaoh's words had left us distraught. No more boys meant no more descendants. We saw his plan clearly: one generation to wipe out the Hebrews. For the Hebrew women would either remain single or intermarry with slaves from other countries, who had also come to Egypt during the famine. If we obeyed these instructions, God's promise to Abraham would come to nothing. We found ourselves key players in a nightmare. To disobey would mean our deaths, and then who would help the Hebrew women in childbirth? Yet to obey was unthinkable—for fear of God, we had to disobey the order whatever the cost. So we continued to pass both baby boys and girls safely into their mothers' arms. What conflicting emotions: the joy of seeing a healthy baby boy, yet the fear of the consequences, and the relief when we delivered a baby girl.

Shiphrah

The day came when we were called before the Egyptian king— we had known that it would only be a matter of time before this happened. We had carefully planned how we would respond to his anger over our disobedience. We would say that the Hebrew women were different from Egyptian women, who often needed much help when giving birth. The Hebrew women gave birth quickly before we arrived, we would explain. To our relief, Pharaoh, already fearing the strength of the Hebrew men, believed us, for would not the Hebrew women also be strong and thus give birth with ease?

We were safe. God had enabled us to speak wisely and we were able to continue our work. Baby boys thrived quietly in their homes and we too were blessed with children.

Puah

Just when we thought that conditions could get no worse, the largest blow was struck. Pharaoh gave all his people the right to throw Hebrew baby boys into the Nile. Shortly after this evil decree, we were called to Jochebed's home. She already had two children, Miriam and Aaron, and a third was well on the way. Before long, with heavy hearts, we placed a fine, healthy child into her arms. 'Is it a boy?' she whispered, looking at us in fear. We nodded and, with tears running down her face, she put the babe to her breast. Her eyes fixed on his, she whispered tenderly, 'What a fine baby; there is something special about him.'

Jochebed

As I held my baby to my breast and gazed into his eyes for that first long look, smelling the sweet scent of my newborn, a strange sensation—no, not a sensation, an understanding—filled me. I *knew* that there was something extraordinary about this baby, that he had the potential to become a remarkable child and an exceptional man. God had purposes for him, I was sure. The tears I had cried on hearing that he was a boy dried on my face.

As the midwives left my home, a plan was already forming in my mind: my baby would not be taken from me and thrown into the Nile; I would hide him. My husband, Amran, was in total accord, and our children, Miriam and Aaron were sworn to secrecy. Our baby thrived on the family's attentiveness, and all too soon his smile of recognition greeted us. I wanted the weeks, days, minutes to stand still, for what would I do when he was older? How would I protect him then? Where could he live in safety?

As the days passed, he became noisier; I knew that our days of keeping him hidden at home were numbered. 'I need a plan, oh Lord God, I need wisdom,' I pleaded. Then it came to me, a place where he would be perfectly safe, where nobody would hear his gurgles and cries: the banks of a secluded part of the river. Hadn't Pharaoh ordered the baby boys to be put in the Nile? We would be obeying his command! So, with Miriam, I collected papyrus reeds and we made a basket, covering the inside with bitumen and pitch in order to make it waterproof. I began by putting Moses in the basket for his sleep, for it was important that he should be accustomed to the smell and sight of the basket. Next we started taking him in the basket down to the river. We chose a quiet place unfrequented by the Hebrew women and placed the basket among the reeds. My son got used to the sounds, sights and gentle movements of the basket bobbing in the water. Eventually I started leaving Miriam on the river bank, trusting her to keep an eye on her brother while I worked at home.

She was there, watching over the basket that contained the sleeping child, on the day that changed all of our lives. I knew that something was amiss when Miriam burst into the house, calling me to come quickly. Fear swept through me; I took her hand and we ran, Miriam breathlessly telling me what had happened. Pharaoh's daughter and her attendants had arrived at the very spot where Miriam had hidden the basket, looking for a private place to bathe. They had come across the basket and opened the lid only to discover our baby who had woken, and faced with a stranger, had started to cry. Pharaoh's daughter had immediately realised that he was a Hebrew baby, but nevertheless had picked him up to console him. My quick-thinking daughter, seeing her brother so distressed, had crept out from her hiding place and had suggested that the baby needed to be fed. Should she fetch a Hebrew woman to nurse him?

I have often wondered whether Pharaoh's daughter guessed that I was his mother as I, trembling, took my child from her arms. My caress and reassuring smile quickly calmed him. Her words simultaneously crushed and uplifted me: she would pay me to nurse and care for him, but would adopt him as soon as he was weaned. My son was to be protected by Pharaoh's daughter – the irony of it: the Egyptian palace would be the safest place for him to grow up. He would have an education, wealth and status, but we would have to part with him. God had prepared the way ahead and given me a few precious years in which to instil in my son his Hebrew identity and teach him that Yahweh was our God: the God almighty;[6] the God who sees;[7] the Everlasting;[8] our Provider.[9]

Reflection and discussion

- Did any words or phrases stand out for you?

- The midwives knew that killing the Hebrew boys would be abhorrent to God. This was long before God gave Moses the command, 'Do not murder' (Exodus 20:13). How do you think they knew this from Hebrew history? Ethical and moral decisions have to be made today where there are no direct biblical references to guide us because the dilemmas did not exist in biblical times. Can you think of any examples? How do we deal with these? It can be particularly difficult when Christians feel strongly but differently to each other on issues. What biblical guidelines do we have?

- Fear of the Israelites' strength led to the Egyptians' cruel behaviour and ruined their ability to live peaceably side by side. Threat, real or imagined, and the desire to protect oneself often seems to bring out the worst in human nature, on a personal, national and international scale. Can you think of examples? Perhaps fear resulting from perceived threat has resulted in behaviour that we have lived to regret and has damaged relationships. If you are able, share such instances. Pray for one another and for national and international situations that have come to mind.

- Shiphrah and Puah give us an example of working lives lived with integrity. Read Colossians 3:23–25. How are these words both an encouragement and a challenge? The work of these midwives and previous biblical midwives was essential in God's plan for his people and humankind. Perez was in the line of Jesus (Matthew

1:3) and Moses was to lead the Hebrews out of Egypt. Our work may be of greater significance than we realise.

- Shiphrah and Puah demonstrated great courage in disobeying Pharaoh's orders and following their consciences. Read Romans 13:1–2. This is the general principle to follow unless the authority and its laws are contrary to God's ways. Then one's conscience must prevail. Share experiences when you have faced a matter of conscience. The consequence of Shiphrah's and Puah's brave decision was massive: saving the Hebrews from ethnic cleansing.

- The midwives showed courage in the way they spoke to Pharaoh. Their shrewd answers saved their lives. Read Matthew 10:19–20. Share times when you have been aware of God giving you the words to say when facing a difficult situation. There may be circumstances in which you need the wisdom to speak with courage and discernment. If you are able, share these and pray for one another.

- The name 'Jochebed' means 'Jehovah is her glory' or 'God's glory'. Jochebed faithfully lived her life for God's glory and taught her children to become people of faith. All three of them played key roles in the history of the Israelites: Moses as leader, Aaron as priest and Miriam as prophetess. What do we mean by the phrase 'living for God's glory'? How do we do this?

- We see Jochebed's sensitivity to God's inner promptings in the way in which she recognised that there was something special about her baby. Share times when you have known that the Lord was prompting you in some way. How can we live with openness and sensitivity in our daily lives?

- Jochebed needed courage to live with each day's uncertainty. She could not see how her child would be kept safe in the future and lived 'one day at a time', trusting God, while taking every precaution on her part to protect her son. Read Jesus' instruction in Matthew 6:34 and Solomon's wise words in Proverbs 3:5–6. What steps can we take to follow this advice?

- Jochebed discovered that God's plan to save her baby was beyond her wildest imagining. Share times when God has answered your prayers in ways that you could not have imagined possible. Meditate on the words, 'Now all glory to God, who is able, through his mighty power at work within us, to accomplish infinitely more than we might ask or think' (Ephesians 3:20).

- Reflect together on the names for God that end this monologue.

Conclusion

Take time to pray through your findings. What might God be saying to you? Is anything particularly relevant to your life at the moment? Write down what you have learnt and refer back to it regularly in the days ahead so that it becomes part of your thinking, reacting and lifestyle.

Deborah

Introduction

- Read Judges 4:1–17; 5:1–3. The details of this account are in Deborah's song in Judges 5. You may like to read all of this chapter in your own time.

- Ask God to speak to you through these episodes. You could use the words from 2 Chronicles 14:11: 'O Lord, no one but you can help the powerless against the mighty! Help us, O Lord our God, for we trust in you alone.'

- Sit back, relax and close your eyes. Imagine the scene as someone reads the monologue.

Monologue

They were dark days for the people of Israel, my people; I longed to comfort them and teach them the ways of the Lord. But they did what was evil in his sight, choosing new gods, and the consequence of that was 20 years of cruel oppression by Jabin, king of Canaan, who reigned from Hazor in the northern territory of Naphtali. Jabin built up his army under the leadership of Sisera until they had 900 iron chariots.

My people lived in fear and seemed to have no fight left in them. They were weak and poor, for traders could no longer use the trade routes safely; those who did still dare to venture south came via small back roads. The fields lay bare. Caught in this poverty trap, the people were unable to rise above their circumstances: they were defeated and desperate.

I say *my* people, for the Lord had brought me into a position of influence and leadership; I was made judge of Israel. My husband Lappidoth and I lived in the hill country of Ephraim, west of the River Jordan. God had given me the gift of prophecy, and the people came to me for counsel, encouragement and when they had disputes that needed to be settled. I worked from under a palm tree between Rama and Bethel, north-west of the Dead Sea. 'Mother of Israel', the people called me.

How I relied on the Lord for wisdom and insight as daily I saw more distress around me, my time in prayer sustaining and strengthening me. I called on the people to come back to the Lord; I urged them to return to God's ways and to seek his face in repentance. I cried out to the Lord to release us from oppression, to raise up leaders, to perform miracles as he had in times gone past. The people needed reminding from our history that large armies and brute force could not prevail against the Lord Almighty; look how God had worked through Moses!

I asked the Lord to provide us with a commander who would have the courage to lead our people against Sisera. He brought to my attention a man named Barak from Kedesh in Naphtali by the south-western shores of the Sea of Galilee, so I sent for him.

When he stood before me I knew that God had been preparing him to lead the Israelites and that Barak was already aware of this. The Lord gave me words of prophecy,

'Has not the Lord commanded you to gather ten thousand men at Mount Tabor from the people of Naphtali and Zebulun? Sisera will meet you by the River Kishon with his chariots and troops and the Lord will give him into your hands.'

Barak seemed reluctant, as had so many of our leaders before him. Finally, he agreed to lead the people, but only if I went with him. I sought the Lord's heart on this and his word came to me, a most astonishing prophecy that was not easy to pass on to Barak: I was to go with him, but Barak would no longer receive the glory for the victory because the Lord would hand Sisera over to a woman.

So it was that my life took an unexpected turn and I found myself travelling to Kedesh to be with the army. Barak called the men to arms and many came from Naphtali and Zebulun; others joined us from the territories of Ephraim, Benjamin, Manasseh and Issachar—10,000 brave men, who offered themselves willingly for the sake of their people. However, no men joined us from Reuben, Gilead, Dan and Asher. Where were they when their brothers needed them? Where were they when the Lord acted in power?

We had but swords and the tools of farmers, for our shields and spears had long since been taken from us by our enemies. While Barak prepared and trained the men, I encouraged and inspired them to be confident in their God.

'Look at what the Lord had done before when his people turned to him. Believe in what he will do again...'

Barak took the tribes to Mount Tabor, ready for the battle to commence. I went with them, waiting on the Lord, asking for his guidance and timing.

Then a day dawned when there was a change in the air and I knew *that* was the day we should fight.

'Go,' I commanded Barak. 'This is the day the Lord has given Sisera into your hands. The Lord is going out before you.'

As Barak started leading the men down from Mount Tabor, the clouds gathered and the heavens opened. The rain began to fall, ever faster and more furiously it came down; thunder and lightning filled the skies. The men marched with courage even though they knew that 900 chariots, with swords protruding from their turning wheels, were heading along the Kishan River towards them, while they did not have even a shield for protection.

The winds howled and the storm raged. The Kishon River quickly overflowed its banks; the hard earth was reduced to mud, the chariots became stuck and some were even washed away by the fast-flowing river. Without their chariots, Sisera's men could not overcome our huge army. As the chariots became trapped in the mire, so the swords in their chariot wheels no longer moved, and our men could attack. Some of Sisera's men attempted to return to Harosheth, but Barak and his men pursued and defeated them. God had enabled us to triumph over our enemies in a way we could never have imagined.

Only one man was not killed by the sword in that battle: Sisera himself. He had fled, only to be killed by a woman, as the Lord had foretold.

That day was the turning point and Israel continued to push harder and harder against Jabin, king of Canaan, until he and his tyranny over my people were destroyed.

Barak and I were given a song by the Lord: a victory song of praise. I sang and taught it to the people, so that generations to come would know what had taken place and how the Lord had given us success.

'Israel's leaders took charge, and the people gladly followed. Praise the Lord!'[1]

We sang of the people, the battle and the woman, Jael, who had killed Sisera.

'Lord, may all your enemies die like Sisera! But may those who love you rise like the sun in all its power!'[2]

Reflection and discussion

- Did any words or phrases stand out for you?

- Like Miriam before her, Deborah was raised up by God to a position of leadership. Deborah's influence was huge: she counselled individuals and tribes, advised politically and spiritually. Deborah saw her role as 'a mother in Israel'—to love, nurture, protect, encourage and challenge the people of God. In this she modelled the words spoken by Jesus in Matthew 23:11, 'The greatest among you must be a servant.' Many others have taken on a 'mothering' role, such as Mother Theresa and Gladys Aylward. Can you think of other examples, famous or known to you, of those who have had a wise and loving influence? What other qualities do you think Deborah displayed that made her such a significant judge/leader?

- Deborah found her God-given identity and purpose: she was Lappidoth's wife, but also a prophetess and leader. It is easy to 'pigeonhole' people into certain roles and hence to limit their development. Who knows what hidden potential lies within a person that can come to fruition given the right opportunities or circumstances? Share times when you have been or felt restrained by others' expectations or when you have discovered potential within yourself to do something new. Read Ephesians 2:10. In what ways does this verse encourage you?

- In the monologue, Deborah interceded for the nation, 'I cried out to the Lord to release us from oppression, to raise up leaders, to perform miracles as he had in times gone past.' How can we play a part in praying for our nation and for spiritual revival? Some individuals seem to have a special calling from God to intercede on behalf of others. Perhaps you sense this calling or know intercessors. Pray for them in this essential role.

- We sense the burden and isolation of leadership in this monologue, and also Deborah's reliance on God. Pray that spiritual leaders, those known to you and those with national and international responsibilities, will be Spirit-filled men and women who walk closely with God. 'Obey your spiritual leaders, and do what they say. Their work is to watch over your souls, and they are accountable to God. Give them reason to do this with joy and not with sorrow' (Hebrews 13:17). Encourage one another by sharing what you have learnt from the example of spiritual leaders.

- Not all the tribes were prepared to join the army (Judges 5:13–18). Some sat 'at home among the sheepfolds' or 'sat unmoved at the seashore', while others 'risked their lives' 'on the heights of the battlefield'. In what ways do we succumb to the temptation to sit back, leaving others to take action? It is easy to play safe and be unadventurous, to paddle, but not go out of our depth. Pray for those who are willing to fight for the freedom of others.

- In wanting Deborah to accompany him, the reluctant Barak revealed that he was more reliant on God's leaders than on God himself. Share times when you have fallen into this trap, or seen it happen. God was gracious to Barak and gave him the support that he requested. However, we see in the narrative that his experience of God's deliverance would be limited; as prophesied by Deborah, Sisera would be killed not by Barak, but by a woman. Are there times when you have felt reluctant to follow God's leading? Why was this? What was the outcome? Other biblical characters showed reluctance in following God's leading. You may like to investigate these in your own time: Gideon (Judges 6:15); Moses (Exodus 4:10–13); Jonah (Jonah 1:1–3; 4:1–2). How are these characters both a challenge and an encouragement to us?

- Deborah eventually accompanied Barak as he led the army against Sisera. Take time to pray for chaplains who, like Deborah, travel with the armed forces and give support in very difficult situations.

- Deborah was a woman of courage: courage to lead in a world dominated by men; courage to pass on God's word even when it was 'uncomfortable' for the listener; courage to take on an unexpected role. Deborah's confidence in God gave her courage, enabling her to encourage and inspire others. She was sensitive to his leading and timing, waiting until the Lord revealed to her that the moment for the army to move forward had come. Share times when sensitivity to God's timing has been crucial for you or when God has given you the courage to take on an unexpected role or speak out for him.

- 'The Lord is with you, a mighty warrior' (Judges 6:12, NIV). 'Do not be terrified; do not be afraid of them. The Lord your God, who is going before you, will fight for you' (Deuteronomy 1:29–30, NIV). Barak's army, ill-equipped but strong in their trust in God, was miraculously able to overcome the mighty army of Sisera because God changed the weather conditions dramatically in their favour. Are you facing 'battles' where the enemy seems strong? Meditate on the above verses and take strength from them. If you are able, share your 'battles' and receive prayerful support.

- The Lord gave his people victory in a way that they could not have imagined. Look back at the prayer at the start of this study. Encourage each other by sharing examples of God's equipping and enabling from your own lives.

Conclusion

Take time to pray through your findings. What might God be saying to you? Is anything particularly relevant to your life at the moment? Write down what you have learnt and refer back to it regularly in the days ahead so that it becomes part of your thinking, reacting and lifestyle.

Jael

Introduction

- Read Judges 4:11, 17–24; 5:24–27.

- Ask God to speak to you through these episodes. You could use the words from 1 Timothy 1:2: 'May God the Father and Christ Jesus our Lord give you grace, mercy and peace.'

- Sit back, relax and close your eyes. Imagine the scene as someone reads the monologue.

Monologue

My husband and I were Kenites, descendants of Moses' father-in-law. The Kenites had always had good relationships with the Israelites, taking their side against their enemies. So imagine my distress when Heber, my husband, told me that our family was to leave the rest of the Kenites and go to Zaanannim, near Kedesh. He reasoned that we needed to separate ourselves from all connections with Israel, for he believed that Israel did not stand a chance against Jabin, king of Canaan. Sisera, Jabin's commander, had developed no less than 900 chariots of iron with swords sticking out of their wheels. The fear of those swords kept the Israelites in terror. It was expedient that we should join the side of Sisera—it was our only hope of survival, or so my husband said. So we left and pitched our tents at Zaanannim, near the huge oak tree.

For 20 years King Jabin had oppressed Israel, and the people had become increasingly poor and weak. The main routes were no longer safe for travel so trade had floundered; only a few brave men were prepared to use the byways into the land. Our family's trade was metal-making and Heber had realised that there was money to be made by selling his skill to Sisera and his army. At least, that was the reason that he gave me for his need to travel to Harosheth-Haggoyim in order to meet with Sisera. But when he gathered all the men from the camp to go with him—our loved ones, husbands, sons, fathers and brothers—I deduced that actually they were going to join Sisera's forces. We had heard that many of the Israelites had gathered near Mount Tabor, forming an army. Our men left, looking determined and serious. My heart ached at the knowledge that Heber had, no doubt, gone to give Sisera details of the Israelite army's whereabouts, and that my husband was, in fact, a traitor. However, although I was saddened by his behaviour, it was against Sisera that my anger burned—this tyrant who used his power to intimidate, bully, impoverish and oppress others, who had turned good men, wanting only to protect their families, like Heber, into traitors.

As we waited for news, clouds gathered in the skies and the rain started to fall; in sheets it came down, softening the ground around our tents where we took shelter, watching and waiting for our men to return.

But no one came, no sound of voices, no beloved faces, just the constant drumming of pelting rain. We started to feel afraid for our men; why gone so long when success had been so sure? At last I saw a man stumbling through the rain into the camp—I ran out to meet him, not caring about getting wet. Which of our family had returned? What was the news? As I neared, I realised that it was not a Kenite; judging by his clothing, it was Sisera, the general, himself. At that moment the awful truth dawned on me: Sisera's army was defeated, our men dead. This man in front of me had left his men; in an act of cowardice he had looked only to his own survival, while leaving his men to die. I loathed this man, hated him with every bone in my body, every muscle and tendon. I held this man personally responsible for the death of the men I loved.

But Sisera did not even have the strength to look into my face, so he failed to see how much I despised him. Although exhausted, his relief at having reached what he considered an ally camp flickered over his face, to be quickly replaced again by fear as he looked back over his shoulder. How I relished his terror, knowing how he had enslaved others with fear. Perhaps I could keep him here and hand him over to the Israelites. Maybe that would make up for my husband's treacherous actions.

It was easy in many ways, for Sisera was expecting my allegiance. In his worn-out state, he quickly succumbed to the invitation to rest in my tent, accepted the rugs that I pulled over him. His shaking subsided and he asked for water. I gave him milk, wanting him to fall into a very deep sleep. Passing the empty skin back to me, he asked me to keep guard at the tent entrance; should anyone pass by, I was to say that no one had come back to the tents. So I stood there, listening to the sound of his breathing getting slower and deeper, until sleep overtook him. How could a man leave his men to die and then sleep like a baby? Such a man did not deserve to live, I thought. I feared that he would wake and leave before I had delivered him over to the Israelites.

To start with that was my plan, but then temptation started to gnaw at me—the man who had abandoned those I loved on the battlefield should die, I mused, but how? 'You must not murder';[1] the commandment within my heart was almost audible. Minutes passed and the internal battle raged. Our men had taken the few weapons that we possessed with them; I was powerless to do anything… or was I? As I stood at the tent door, my eyes fixed on one of the tent pegs; I could use that. I was strong from years of putting up and taking down tents, so I did not doubt my ability. 'Do not seek revenge.'[2] Who had spoken? But the fear returned—Sisera might wake and escape—and the battle within me was lost.

I pulled the peg up easily from the soft ground. If anything, anger and agitation had increased my strength. Taking a hammer, I approached Sisera. Not a stir. I knelt down beside him; still no movement. I fixed my eyes on the target: his temple. I lifted the peg over it and with one immense blow, hammered the peg into his head. It was done. He died instantly. I sat there, unable to move, watching the blood flow from his wound.

I am not sure how much time passed, but I became aware that the rain had stopped and of shouts outside. Leaving the tent, I walked in the direction of the commotion; our women were surrounded by Israelites, and Barak, their leader, was among them.

'I know why you are here,' I said to him. 'Come with me and I will show you the man you are looking for.'

Barak followed me to my tent and there he gazed down at Sisera, the tent peg still in his temple. Then Barak turned to me and I heard him acknowledge in a quiet voice,

'The honour is not mine, for the Lord has given Sisera into the hands of a woman.'

Reflection and discussion

- Did any words or phrases stand out for you?

- Jael's husband, Heber, chose expediency and self-interest. He decided to collaborate with the enemy in the hope of saving himself and his family. Many have chosen such a route and the decision must be a hard one: protecting oneself and loved ones, or serving a higher cause. What instances of this can you think of from history? We may face choices between self-interest and a higher cause, but on a smaller scale. Can you give some examples of such challenges that you have faced or may face?

- In the monologue, Jael, although having no choice but to pitch her tent where her husband had decided, maintained an inward loyalty to the Israelites. This cannot have been easy for her; it must have taken courage. You may find yourself in situations where you are surrounded by those who hold different values or beliefs to you. If appropriate, share these and pray for one another. Many Christians throughout the world are forced to live with a faith that cannot be expressed openly, and are secretly maintaining an inner loyalty to God. Are there organisations that could help you to pray meaningfully for such people?

- Fear had bound the Israelites for many years, keeping them from taking action. Do we have fears that curb our lives? These may be severe, such as phobias, or more minor ones, but nevertheless limiting. If you are able, share these and give each other support. Read and meditate on Isaiah 41:10. In the Bible, the words 'Do not be afraid' are spoken over and over again to people who *were* afraid, not to make them guilty for experiencing fear, but to encourage them to persevere and take action in spite of their fear, assured of God's presence.

- In the monologue we see Jael's internal struggle. God's laws are clear, 'You must not murder' (Exodus 20:13) and 'Do not seek revenge' (Leviticus 19:18), but Jael chose to take the law into her own hands. Read Paul's words in Romans 12:19–21. These refer back to Leviticus 19:18 and Proverbs 25:21–22. How can we apply these verses to situations that we meet in our everyday lives?

- The Bible tells us that we all face temptation. In Matthew 4 we see Jesus responding to temptation by using verses of scripture to counteract and overcome each temptation. He teaches us in the Lord's Prayer to pray that we will not succumb when tempted. In 1 Corinthians 10:13, we read, 'God is faithful. He will not allow the temptation to be more than you can stand. When you are tempted, he will show you a way out so that you can endure.' What are the temptations that we face? What 'ways out' have you experienced? When we do give way to temptation, we have the promise in 1 John 1:9, 'But if we confess our sins to him, he is faithful and just to forgive us our sins and cleanse us from all wickedness.'

- Jael had a physical strength and mental strength that matched the challenging situation she faced. Share times when this has been your experience. Meditate on the following verses, 'Your strength will equal your days' (Deuteronomy 33:25, NIV), and 'The Lord is my strength and my song; he has become my salvation' (Psalm 118:14, NIV).

- Jael's action took courage, for there was risk involved—it could have all gone terribly wrong for her, with Sisera waking at the crucial moment. Have there been times when you have chosen to take a courageous step, in spite of the risks? Perhaps you need to make a decision which is leaving you feeling vulnerable. If you feel able, ask for prayer support.

- In the lives of the Israelite people we see a cycle that they often repeated: rebellion against God and failure; calling on the Lord for help and forgiveness; God's grace and salvation. If we are honest, we are only too familiar with this cycle in our own lives. Encourage one another by sharing how God has poured grace into your life when you have called on him. In your own time you may like to read Paul's words in Romans 7:14—8:4, describing his struggle with sin and its remedy in Jesus Christ and the power of the 'life-giving Spirit'.

Conclusion

Take time to pray through your findings. What might God be saying to you? Is anything particularly relevant to your life at the moment? Write down what you have learnt and refer back to it regularly in the days ahead so that it becomes part of your thinking, reacting and lifestyle.

Jephthah's Daughter

Introduction

- Read Judges 11:29–38. (You may like to read all of Judges 11.)

- Ask God to speak to you through these episodes. You could use the words from 2 Thessalonians 2:16–17: 'Now may our Lord Jesus Christ himself and God our Father, who loved us and by his grace gave us eternal comfort and a wonderful hope, comfort you and strengthen you in every good thing you do and say.'

- Sit back, relax and close your eyes. Imagine the scene as someone reads the monologue.

Monologue

'He's coming!' came the shout. I had been waiting with my drum, practising the celebratory dance that I had learnt, for my father had led the Israelites from Gilead to fight the Ammonites, who had made war against us, and the Israelites had defeated them. This was his homecoming and I was full of excitement. My father is a great warrior and I have always adored him. I am his only daughter, indeed his only child; he calls me the apple of his eye.

We have been living in Gilead for a relatively short period of time, previously living east in the land of Tob. My father spoke little of his childhood and family, but I had gleaned that he was the offspring of a man named Gilead and a prostitute. My grandfather had brought up my father with his wife's sons, and all had gone smoothly while they were young. However, once they fully realised the situation, the brothers turned against my father, not wanting him to have any part in the inheritance. Perhaps, too, they were envious of his physical prowess. Finally, they drove him away and my father settled in Tob. A born leader, he had gathered followers around him in Tob. Some of these men made me nervous: they were so rough. That was the environment in which I grew up and where I thought I would live out my life.

But we left that life behind us, for when the Ammonites waged war on Israel, it was to my father that the elders of Gilead turned. They knew that there was no one like him to lead them and to win men's loyalty, for not only was he an outstanding warrior, he was also a great strategist and negotiator. 'Talk first' was his motto, and if that failed, take strong action. My father loved to recount how the elders had begged him to come back and be their leader and how he had reminded them of the way he had been treated by his family in the past. How could they expect him to lead men into battle when they had driven him away? He made a bargain with them: if he did as they wished and the Lord gave them the victory, he would remain their leader after the fighting was over. Of course they had to agree, so desperate were they for his help.

When we had arrived in Gilead, my father's leadership was proclaimed before God. At first he tried to avoid further fighting by reasoning with the Ammonites, but to no avail. He believed that they were in the wrong and he was justified in fighting them. The Lord would judge between them.

So this homecoming was more than a victory for Israel, it was a personal triumph for my father, who was now judge of Israel, leader of the very people who had rejected him. How thrilled I was when I saw my father in the distance! I rushed out of the house beating my drum, my laughter and singing mingling, as I performed my triumphant dance. How delighted he would be to see me twirl and spin, and to know the luxuries of home life once again after the deprivations of warfare!

As our eyes met, a look of horror came over his face and a strangled cry came from his throat. With one strong movement he tore his clothes and fell to the floor. I stopped singing and ran to him. What could have happened to cause him such great and sudden distress?

'Oh my beloved daughter, you have taken me to the depths of despair. You have brought calamity on me. For I have promised the Lord and I cannot go back on my word,' he wept as he spoke.

'Father, tell me, what is it? What can I possibly have done?' I asked in confusion, tears falling down my face as I knelt beside him. His sobs were violent, wracking his body. What had reduced my warrior father to this?

'Tell me, tell me,' I urged.

The truth emerged: my father had experienced the Spirit of the Lord coming upon him and in his exhilaration he had vowed to the Lord that, if the Lord gave him victory over the Ammonites, whatever came through the door to meet him on his return from war would be sacrificed as a burnt offering.

'And it was me,' I whispered in horror, 'not an animal, it was me.' I fell into his arms and we wept together. 'Oh father, oh father,' I groaned.

I took his anguished face in my hands and spoke to him falteringly between our sobs. For those few minutes our roles were reversed as I comforted the man who had always comforted me, as I sought to strengthen the man who had always given me strength.

My words came out slowly as I attempted to maintain my control. 'Father, you have made a vow to the Lord—and he has given you victory over the Ammonites—you must keep your side of the bargain—for look how the Lord has enabled us to be a land at peace. I am the price that must be paid for that peace. But first—let me go with my friends up into the mountains for two months—let us weep together for all that will never be—for the marriage I will not have—for the children I will never bear. Let us grieve for the experiences that we will never share together. I need time—time to be with them—time to come to terms with this reality—so that when I come back, I can go to my death with resolution.'

He has agreed, and here I am, preparing the little I will need to take. My friends, who have become sisters to me since we moved to Gilead, are doing the same in their homes. We will meet soon; we will know freedom and friendship; we will laugh and weep together and I will leave them with precious memories. I will prepare myself, then return and go willingly to my death, sparing my father the agony of seeing me being dragged to the altar. I am terrified. I will be terrified. I will want to run and hide, but I will not... God be my help.

Footnote

We end the monologue here. Jephthath's daughter does as she promised her father: 'When she returned home, her father kept the vow he had made, and she died a virgin' (Judges 11:39). Many scholars believe from these words that he therefore went through with his vow. This view is supported by the fact that a lament commemorated this event: 'the daughters of Israel went year by year to lament the daughter of Jephthah the Gileadite four days in the year' (Judges 11:40, ESV). Human sacrifice was forbidden to the Israelites.[1] However, many of the surrounding cultures practised this terrible custom. The book of Judges records how the Lord's people displeased him greatly by taking on the customs of the nations around them. There was a steady moral deterioration; the book of Judges concluding with the words, 'Everyone did what was right in their own eyes' (Judges 21:25, ESV). On the other hand, there are scholars who interpret the sacrifice as figurative, believing that Jephthah's daughter was not killed but instead had to remain a virgin and thus sacrificed becoming a mother, meaning that Jephthah's line came to an end. They believe that Jephthah, knowing Israel's history and laws, would not have gone as far as a literal sacrifice.

Reflection and discussion

- Did any words or phrases stand out for you?

- It was a custom for the women to dance when the men returned from victorious battles. It was one of the few occasions when women could dance and sing in public. What role does celebration play in our personal, church and community lives? Are there ways we could engage in celebratory activities as a means of drawing people together?

- Jephthah's daughter showed immense courage when she discovered what her father had vowed. Her response is immediate in the biblical narrative: God had given the Israelites victory, so her father should keep his vow. There are many people who suffer, even to the point of death, because of the foolish or deluded decisions of others. Often these are the more vulnerable members of society. Can you think of examples? Many women are powerless and therefore abused in different ways across the world. Bring these people and situations to God in prayer.

- Jephthah's daughter's courage was also shown in the way that she approached death. She wanted to have some say in what she saw as the inevitable and so asked for two months to enjoy the beauty and freedom of the countryside and the joy of friendship, to remember what had been and to prepare herself for what was to come. She wanted time to grieve the experiences that she would never have, so that when death came she could face it with resignation. Share your reactions to her courage. What does she teach us about facing our own mortality?

- The Bible indicates that vows are to be taken seriously and should not be made except after careful consideration. Read Numbers 30:1–2 and Deuteronomy 23:21. Jesus implies that vows are not really necessary if we are living as people of integrity, for our 'yes' or 'no' should be sufficient. Read Jesus' words taken from the Sermon on the Mount in Matthew 5:33–37. What do you think Jesus meant by the words, 'Simply let your "Yes" be "Yes" and your "No", "No"; anything beyond this comes from the evil one'? (v. 37, NIV)

- James warns us to be careful what we say. Read James 1:26 and 3:2–12. We need to guard against being impulsive or foolish in our speech and watch what we verbally commit ourselves to so that we can be people of our word. In what practical ways can we follow this advice? Read Ephesians 4:29 and 31.

- Jephthah's daughter knew her father's strengths and weaknesses, his bitterness, his leadership skills, his military expertise, his ambition and his folly, yet she still showed respect for the promise that he had made to the Lord. This was a 'love [that] covers a multitude of sins' (1 Peter 4:8). What does respecting and honouring people look like in practice?

- If only Jephthah had realised that the Lord, who is full of mercy, desired him to be merciful. Being obedient to his laws and having a contrite heart were far more important to God than burnt offerings and sacrifices. Read 1 Samuel 15:22 and Psalm 51:16–17. What do these verses have to say to us today?

- Jephthah failed to understand the nature of the God he worshipped—a God who is much more interested in our care for others than our rigid following of regulations. How do we perceive God? How does this reflect in our attitude to him, ourselves and others? Read Ephesians 4:32. Perhaps we, like Jephthah, fail to recognise God's desire and power to give us a fresh start. Read Isaiah 1:18. During the week take time to meditate on Psalm 103:7–18, praying that God will reveal his character more and more to you.

- Jephthah tried to bargain with God: if God gave him the victory, he would sacrifice whatever came out of his home first. The result was tragic for him. We cannot bargain with God. In what ways have we been, or are we, tempted to do this, even if only subconsciously? God tells us through the prophet Jeremiah to, 'Ask for the old, godly way, and walk in it. Travel its path and you will find rest for your souls' (Jeremiah 6:16). What do you understand by 'the old, godly way'?

- The friends of Jephthah's daughter both comforted her and grieved with her. Why is it important to follow the command to 'mourn with those who mourn' (Romans 12:15, NIV)? An annual four-day remembrance was set up for young Israelite women to go away to 'lament the fate of Jephthah's daughter' (Judges 11:40). How can we both give and receive support on the anniversaries of sad occasions in our lives?

Conclusion

Take time to pray through your findings. What might God be saying to you? Is anything particularly relevant to your life at the moment? Write down what you have learnt and refer back to it regularly in the days ahead so that it becomes part of your thinking, reacting and lifestyle.

Michal (Part 1)

Introduction

- Read 1 Samuel 18:6–30; 19:9–18. You may like to read the verses from 1 Samuel 18 before the monologue and the verses from 1 Samuel 19 afterwards.

- Ask God to speak to you through this episode. You could use the words from Philippians 1: 11: 'May you always be filled with the fruit of your salvation—the righteous character produced in your life by Jesus Christ—for this will bring much glory and praises to God.'

- Sit back, relax and close your eyes. Imagine the scene as someone reads the monologue.

Monologue

To say that I was in love with David was an understatement: I adored the very ground he walked on. I was not the only one in my family who loved David—my elder brother, Jonathan, had a profound friendship with him and deep loyalty to him. I knew that David had married me in order to unite the tribes of Israel and Judah, but I had hoped that he would come to love me and did all in my power to bring that about. But something held him back from me—perhaps he could never quite trust me; after all, when it came to the crunch, where would my allegiance lie: with him or with King Saul, my father? The king was to become threatened by both Jonathan's and my commitment to David.

A great change took place in my father after Samuel, the prophet, had warned him that he had been rejected by God as king because he had not followed the Lord's commands.[1] My father became a tormented man and we all suffered the consequences. The sense of well-being that we had seen in him, through the Spirit of the Lord's anointing, had gone; he had fits of rage and times of deep depression. We were in despair as to know how to help him. It was one of the servants who came up with a solution: find a young man talented in playing the lyre, who could soothe my father when distressed with the sheer beauty of his playing. My father agreed and a search for a suitable musician began. That was when David came into our lives. One of the servants had reported that he had found an ideal person, the son of Jesse from Bethlehem, called David. Not only was he a skilful musician, he was handsome, strong, brave and wise beyond his age. Moreover, the servant reported that David was a godly man and that the Lord was with him.[2]

Initially, David was a great success with my father; whenever he was in anguish, David's music calmed and refreshed him. Saul's trust in David grew and it wasn't long before my father had requested that David stay with him permanently, first giving him the position of armour-bearer and then a high rank in leading the army. Although Jonathan and I loved David all the more, my father began to grow jealous of him, for it was evident that everyone, both in and out of the king's palace, admired David more than Saul.

'Saul has struck down his thousands and David his tens of thousands,' they sang.

From the moment that my father heard those words, he started to plot against David. Imagine my distress when I learned that my father had offered my elder sister, Merab, to David in marriage. Jonathan and I guessed what was behind this plan: David would receive Merab in return for giving his loyalty to the king, and for fighting valiantly; our father would send David out against the Philistines, whom he knew were determined to take revenge on David for the part he had played in defeating them. However, David refused to marry Merab, insisting that his origins were too humble for him to be made the king's son-in-law. Eventually, much to my relief, Merab was given in marriage to Adriel of Meholah.

It was my chance—a few carefully chosen words to my maidservants, who would pass on what I said to the other servants, and in time my father himself would know that I loved David. The king was pleased when he learnt of my passion for his perceived rival and once again asked David to become his son-in-law. I learnt that my father had instructed his servants to tell David just how much the king delighted in him, how it was the king's wish for him to become his son-in-law and how much David was loved by all in the palace. Still David refused on the grounds of being unworthy. Then my father concocted a devilish plan: David would pay a bride price and possibly... probably... die in the process. The price: the foreskins of 100 Philistines. David accepted the challenge and a date was set for the bride price to be paid. Foolishly, I imagined that he loved me and was taking on this challenge to win me. I was to learn bitterly that the lure for David was not the love of the king's daughter, but the thought of becoming the king's son-in-law. No wonder my father was so delighted at the idea of me marrying David, for having David in a high-profile position would make him even more of a target for the Philistines. What should I have expected—that my father cared for my personal happiness? I should have known that my father would always have his own agenda.

When David went to battle, I waited. Petrified that I would lose the man I loved, I swung between fear and hope—a hope fed by the memories of David's previous victories. Finally, news spread through the palace that David had been seen returning triumphantly—I was to marry David! Those were the happiest days of my life, preparing for marriage and becoming David's wife. They were also days of great success for David; each time the Philistines came to fight against us, David succeeded in pushing them back. Everyone grew to love the very sound of his name.

However, the period of joy was short-lived. The king became even more envious of David's achievements and popularity; my father was afraid, for he knew that God was with David. Once his plots to have David killed by the Philistines failed, he started to make his own plans, which he disclosed to Jonathan and his servants.[3] In marrying David I had a choice: loyalty to my king and father or loyalty to the man I loved, my husband. Jonathan had the same choice: Saul or David. We both chose David.

Initially, Jonathan was able to maintain peace, but history repeated itself in the form of more successes for David in battle, which further fuelled my father's jealousy. He attempted to kill David, hurling a spear at my husband while he was playing the harp. David dodged out of the way and ran. He burst into our house, sweat pouring from his face. It was no good; there could never be peace between Saul and David. I looked from my top window and saw men waiting by our door to capture my husband. How could he escape?

'David, the moment you leave the house tomorrow you will be killed. You need to flee tonight,' I urged.

We had to act quickly—we tied ropes from an upstairs window, choosing one as far from the entrance as possible, then I let David down, saw him jump to the ground and run for his life. I clung to the hope that my father's rage would decrease and that my husband would be able to return. Perhaps Jonathan could once again speak to the king on David's behalf. Meanwhile, I needed to give David as much time as possible to flee. What if my father ordered his men to enter our home to fetch David? I put a statue in our bed, covered it with David's clothes and sheets, a goat's hair pillow at its head. Then I waited for dawn, trying to snatch some sleep, but my thoughts were with David; imagining him running under the cover of darkness. I asked God to keep him safe.

Light was barely upon us when I heard the sound of knocks on the door, a servant scrambling to respond, footsteps on the stairs and the knock on my bedroom door that I had been expecting. Heart beating fast, I got up.

'Move slowly, speak quietly, play for time,' I told myself.

'Is my father asking for David?' I enquired. 'He will be unable to come to the king. He is ill, too ill even to walk; he's resting now.'

They followed my glance to the supposedly sleeping David. I saw the men's dilemma: to push past the king's daughter into our bedroom, or to disobey the king. Perhaps they, like many others in the palace, secretly supported David. Perhaps they were glad to return empty-handed to the king. Even now perhaps my father's temper would cool. But no, it was not long before they returned. However, this time they hurried past me, entering our room, pulling back the covers on our bed. I stood dignified and silent as they discovered my deception. They rushed past me back to the king. I waited for the inevitable—to be called before my father. I planned my defence.

'Why have you helped my enemy to escape? Why have you deceived your father?' the king ranted.

To say 'because I love David' was too dangerous; if I was going to survive, I had to speak carefully.

'I had no choice. He made me let him go. He would have killed me if I had done anything to prevent him.'

My father looked at me coldly and with distrust, but my words were enough to save my life.

Reflection and discussion

- Did any words or phrases stand out for you?

- In this monologue we see Michal making some life-changing choices: she chose to make sure that her father knew of her love for David, and she chose loyalty to her husband over loyalty to the king (see this principle in Genesis 2:24). This took great courage, for she knew that her father's reactions were erratic and what the consequences could have been for her. Have you ever found yourself pulled in two directions by conflicting loyalties or demands? How did you deal with this? How do we work out a system of priorities? Does this need to be reviewed from time to time? Can you think of advice in the Bible that helps us when setting priorities?

- In the biblical account there is no indication that Michal's love for David is reciprocated by him. Pray for those whose lives have been blighted by unrequited love or unfaithfulness. Meditate on the words from Psalm 34:18 (NIV), 'The Lord is close to the broken-hearted and saves those who are crushed in spirit', and on the words from Isaiah 42:3 (NIV), 'A bruised reed he will not break, and a smouldering wick he will not snuff out.'

- We see in the Bible the important place music holds in praise and celebration. In this monologue we see the power of music to sooth and heal. What music has this effect on you? We may bring songs of lament to the Lord as well as songs of praise. Read Psalm 5:1-3.

- Both Saul and David received a powerful anointing of the Spirit (1 Samuel 10:9-10 and 16:13). However, Saul, although a young man of great promise, did not obey the Lord and then tried to cover up his disobedience, leading to God rejecting him as king (1 Samuel 15). He had thought that he could get away with appearing to follow God fully and yet only obeying him partially. This is a warning to us not to grieve the Holy Spirit, but to seek to live with integrity. Read Ephesians 4:30 and 5:15. Can you suggest small, and larger, ways in which we may seemingly be following the Lord, but yet are not walking in his ways? Read Jesus' words in Matthew 23:23-28. What are our modern-day equivalents? Pray for each other and for those in positions where their lack of integrity can have a huge knock-on effect on others.

- In contrast, David enjoyed God's blessing and favour with the people. Share ways in which you have experienced the Lord's favour. Reflecting on this story, how do we find favour with God? God's grace (his undeserved favour) is a gift. As a response to his grace, we then do 'those things that lead to holiness and result in eternal life' (Romans 6:22). What 'things' 'lead to holiness'?

- At the end of this narrative, Michal's reply to Saul, although not true, protected her from his wrath, which she knew only too well could turn to violence. Pray for those who have to constantly watch their words in order to avoid angry and violent reactions.

Conclusion

Take time to pray through your findings. What might God be saying to you? Is anything particularly relevant to your life at the moment? Write down what you have learnt and refer back to it regularly in the days ahead so that it becomes part of your thinking, reacting and lifestyle.

Michal (Part 2)

Introduction

- Read 1 Samuel 25:42–44; 2 Samuel 3:12–18; 2 Samuel 6:12–23. You may like to read the verses from 2 Samuel 6 after the monologue.

- Ask God to speak to you through this episode. You could use the words from Colossians 4:3: 'Pray... that God will give us many opportunities to speak about his mysterious plan concerning Christ.'

- Sit back, relax and close your eyes. Imagine the scene as someone reads the monologue.

Monologue

That night was the last time that I was to see David for some years. By helping him to escape, I had in effect lost both my father and my husband. Time passed slowly and with little purpose. Eventually, word came to me from my father that I was to be given in marriage to Paltiel, son of Laish from Gallim. It was pointless to weep: I knew that I had no choice but to obey.

The blow when I heard that David had taken two women, Abigail and Ahinoam, as his wives was one from which I never fully recovered. His revenge on my father was great: the king had given me to another man, so he would take other wives. I was heartbroken, for my image of a perfect David was shattered; my love for him started to crumble and slowly died.

The struggle between David and my father continued, David ever gaining in strength and the king only weakening. Then came the day when my father and three of my brothers were killed in battle.[1] I grieved for Jonathan, my beloved brother, and for my father, in spite of the misery he had caused me. I knew that David would be mourning too.[2]

In the course of time, news reached me that David was established as king over Judah in Hebron and had taken more wives, Maacah, Haggith, Abital and Eglah,[3] and in so doing had made truces with the neighbouring kingdoms. These women were signs of his personal power, their sons a sign of his future kingdom. Bitter and barren, I despaired.

Until one day, Ish-bosheth, another of my brothers, sent word to me. I was ordered to return to David, who had claimed his right to me, his first wife. I knew I was but a means for David to negotiate and strengthen his claim as ruler over all of Israel; I was the confirmation that he had a rightful place in Saul's house. Ish-bosheth's commander-in-chief, Abner, came for me. Paltiel had loved me; I had received respect and known both kindness and peace in his household. Now these, too, were to be torn from me. He followed me, weeping. I had no tears left; they had all been shed long ago. I had only my dignity and a new hope, for I was David's first wife and no one could take that position away from me. Moreover, if I bore David a son, he would be king one day.

Finally, Abner turned to Paltiel and commanded roughly, 'Go home!' Paltiel could not fight against his authority; he turned and went.

So I lived in Hebron watching David become ever more powerful; in time he was made king of all Israel. My husband was 30 years old. We remained in Hebron for a further seven and a half years and then David ordered Joab, his commander, to take Jebus, the fortified city of the Jebusites. When it was conquered, it was renamed the city of David, the stronghold of Zion: Jerusalem.[4] My husband had a sumptuous palace built for all his wives and children. But in my part of the palace, there were no children; I grieved deeply.

David took more wives and concubines, signs of his influence and authority, and many more children were born to him.[5] My resentment grew; I had adored David, but he had never loved me in return. I had been no more than David's attempt at peace with my father, never more than a way for David to establish a place in Saul's household.

The competition between the women in the palace was intense and the children sensed this, imbibed it, took ownership of it. I watched them grow up, observing the mounting hatred each child had for the others. So I retreated, spending more time at the window in my bedroom, sitting looking out of the palace and over Jerusalem, watching the city extend.

David believed strongly that the Ark of the Covenant, the symbol of God's presence, should now be in Jerusalem. However, it was a while before the Ark was to be brought into the city.[6] When my husband realised that blessings would come to Jerusalem if the Ark of the Covenant was within the city walls, he made plans to retrieve it. What celebrations were arranged for that day!

I heard them before I saw them, such shouting, singing and music: the sounds of horns, lyres harps, tambourines, flutes, castanets and cymbals—such raucous, jubilant celebration. Then the crowds of rejoicing people came into view; but I had no part in it, for I felt no joy in my heart. Who was that at the front jumping wildly and exuberantly? I judged by his simple linen tunic that it was one of the priests. To my horror, as they neared, I recognised that it was actually David making an exhibition of himself before the whole city, neither dressed like a king, nor behaving like a king—how could he act in such a way? I despised him.

I saw the Ark of the Covenant being carried into the tent which had been pitched for the occasion. However, it was many hours before

I saw my husband. I heard the continued celebrations and learned that David had offered burnt offerings and peace offerings before the Lord; the king had blessed the people, providing a celebration feast of bread, meat, date and raisin cakes for every man, woman and child in the city. Eventually the noise diminished as people started to go home and I heard that David was returning to bless our household. From the moment I had seen him prancing through the streets, I had been planning how to greet him. In the hollowness of my heart, I realised that the man I had once loved so deeply, I now regarded as ridiculous. Oh, in spite of the hurt I had suffered at David's hands, the rejection and the nagging pain of unrequited love, I had still admired his skills as a soldier, leader and king; I had admired his strength and appearance. But now that I no longer respected him, I was left with nothing but scorn for him. Respect, although a poor substitute for love, had been sufficient to maintain some sort of relationship between us.

I went out to meet him, for I could hold in my words no longer.

'How the King of Israel has distinguished himself today,' I said with bitter sarcasm, 'taking off his robe in front of servant girls, behaving like any vulgar fellow.'

There was a long silence as David took in my words and the expression on my face. Eventually he spoke,

'It was before the Lord that I danced to celebrate, the Lord who chose me over your father and his household, the Lord who appointed me king of Israel. Your words will not stop me worshipping in this way, even if I were to feel foolish myself, even if I were to debase myself further in your eyes. However, you are wrong: the servant girls do not look down on me, on the contrary, they honour me.'

I know now that one sentence can destroy a relationship and extinguish hope. I had spoken words that never should have been uttered, that could never be erased from the memory of either the speaker or the listener. Who was I, who had been shown mercy by David in spite of my father's many attempts to kill him, to judge? Who was I to criticise the worship of another, one who had, since his youth, sung songs to the Lord and made music to him? The Lord had sought a man after his own heart and had chosen my husband, David.[7] Who was I to despise him?

David never came to me again and I never bore the child I had so longed for.

Reflection and discussion

- Did any words or phrases stand out for you?

- Michal, in doing the right thing and enabling David to escape, lost her relationship with both him and her father. She became a cog in a political wheel, first given away in marriage by her father and then claimed back by David. She must have felt used and must have suffered greatly. Taking the 'right' course of action in a situation can require courage. It can result in blessing, but can also result in hardship, even death. Can you think of examples from your life and the lives of others that illustrate this? Read Jesus' words in Matthew 5:10–12, which promise an eventual blessing.

- Michal needed courage to live with the enforced changes in her life: the departure of David, her marriage to Paltiel, the return to David. Share times when you have been on the receiving end of enforced change. What helped you to adapt?

- In the monologue, Michal's love for David slowly disintegrated. Initially deeply in love with him, she put him on a pedestal, and as she became disillusioned with the actual man that she discovered him to be, her love and then, finally, her respect died. Placing others or allowing oneself to be put on a pedestal is dangerous, 'for everyone has sinned; we all fall short of God's glorious standard' (Romans 3:23). The higher the pedestal, the further there is to fall. If you are able, share times you have experienced this or seen it happen. Pray for those who have 'fallen from a pedestal', and for those who have known the pain of their love for another disintegrating in the face of a harsh reality. Pray that bitterness will not take root.

- In the monologue, Michal's despair turned to bitterness as David took more wives who bore him sons, while she remained childless. The Bible indicates that we 'allow' bitterness to take root within us, and that we are responsible for helping each other not to respond to life's blows with bitterness, 'Look after each other so that none of you fails to receive the grace of God. Watch out that no poisonous root of bitterness grows up to trouble you, corrupting many' (Hebrews 12:15). Are there situations where we have become, or now risk becoming, bitter? Could this be alleviated or prevented by seeking support from others? In your own time meditate on the words in Ephesians 4:31–32.

- Michal became resentful when she thought of the ways in which she had been used by her husband and father. How does resentment damage us and others? Do we hold resentments against others, even against God? If you are able, share these and pray for one another.

- Most of David's children grew up to be full of jealousy and hatred. Children learn their values and patterns of behaviour by observing and listening to those closest to them. Think of those children in your sphere of influence and how you can positively contribute to their development. Share your ideas.

- Michal eventually lost all respect for David. She failed to 'guard her heart'. In Proverbs 4:23 we read, 'Guard your heart above all else, for it determines the course of your life.' Read Jesus' words in Luke 6:45. Out of the overflow of Michal's heart streamed words that caused permanent damage to her relationship with David.

It was a tragic ending to her story and a stark warning to us. We need God's inward transformation, 'Let God transform you into a new person by changing the way you think' (Romans 12:2). How have you been aware of this inner transformation and its effect on the way you think and speak?

- David worshipped God from his heart and without inhibition; those who recognised this, such as the servant girls, understood. Throughout the world people respond to God in very different ways, from exuberant praise to silent contemplation. How do you express your inner joy in worship? We all have styles of worship that we are more comfortable with. What influences this? How are we in danger of behaving like Michal, or quenching the Holy Spirit (1 Thessalonians 5:19, ESV)? It is easy to be influenced by the worship of others. How can we be sincere in our responses to God?

- The Lord chose David as a 'man after his own heart' (1 Samuel 13:14) to be part of his 'mysterious plan concerning Christ' (see the opening prayer). What do you think is meant by the phrases in italics?

Conclusion

Take time to pray through your findings. What might God be saying to you? Is anything particularly relevant to your life at the moment? Write down what you have learnt and refer back to it regularly in the days ahead so that it becomes part of your thinking, reacting and lifestyle.

Abigail (Part 1)

Introduction

- Read 1 Samuel 25:1–42. You may like to read verses 1–22 before the monologue and the remaining verses after it.

- Ask God to speak to you through this episode. You could use the words from Hebrews 13:21: 'May he produce in you, through the power of Jesus Christ, every good thing that is pleasing to him. All glory to him forever and ever! Amen.'

- Sit back, relax and close your eyes. Imagine the scene as someone reads the monologue.

Monologue

Samuel, our great prophet, had died and all Israel grieved his passing. My husband Nabal, however, remained absorbed in his own affairs, promoting his ever-increasing wealth. His business was in Carmel, south of Hebron, and he controlled much of the pastureland in the surrounding area, owning 3000 sheep and 1000 goats. Such a successful man might well have held his wife's respect, but I knew how badly my husband treated people; he was surly and showed no generosity in his dealings with others. The high-ranking position he maintained locally was preserved partly by his descent from Caleb, who had spied out Canaan with Joshua, and by the fear which he evoked in others. I needed my resourcefulness to keep the peace as much as possible both within the household and with our neighbours. What was the use of the beauty and wisdom that I had been blessed with if I did not draw on them to maintain good relationships?

After Samuel's death, I heard that David and his men had left the stronghold at Masada to come and dwell in the wilderness around Paran. No doubt David feared that King Saul would renew his pursuit now that the restraining influence of Samuel and his prophecies had gone. Our shepherds reported that their arrival had benefited us, for David and his men had acted as a protection both for them and the flocks. We had therefore enjoyed better returns for our labour than ever before. Not once had David's men taken advantage of us by helping themselves to our lambs.

It was sheep-shearing time and Nabal was overseeing the work, ensuring through any means that we got the best price for our fleeces. The first I knew of the trouble my husband had caused us was when one of our young shepherds arrived at our home requesting an audience with me. Surprised, I agreed. I had always made sure that I listened to our servants, whatever rank they held within the household. It was my way of keeping informed and of being in a position to promote everybody's well-being.

What he told me horrified me. David had sent ten young men to request whatever food Nabal could make available so that they could hold a feast. He had wished our household peace, asking for what was quite reasonable in view of the protection he had given us. Yet my husband had refused and had not shown the hospitality that was expected of him. Worse than that, my husband's response has been both insulting and proud; it was bound to have incurred David's wrath.

I had heard enough of David to know that he would retaliate quickly. There was no time to be lost; I had to think clearly and take immediate action. I issued a string of instructions and soon the servants were in a frenzy of activity: preparing donkeys, packing on to their backs 200 loaves, two skins of wine, five prepared sheep, grain, 100 raisin cakes and 200 fig cakes. No message of our action was to be sent to Nabal; he must remain ignorant for fear of his likely foolish response. Did the man not realise that David's men could slaughter us all?

It was not enough to send these gifts; I must go with them and do all in my power to pacify David. I sent the young servant ahead, telling him that I myself would follow with the other servants and donkeys, instructing him to advise me as to David's whereabouts.

My young servant performed this task, returning to tell me that David was approaching fast, for he had determined that he would leave no one in Nabal's household alive; by morning we would be massacred.

My fear mounted with every step that my donkey took, but I was resolute: we must try to make a treaty. As soon as I saw David, my heart went cold. There must have been several hundred armed men accompanying him. I climbed quickly down, telling the servants to wait with the laden donkeys.

David called his men to stop their approach. A silence fell as I hurried forward and fell to the ground before him, my head bowed low. I sensed his surprise: a woman coming out to make peace!

'My Lord, please listen to what I have to say. Blame me! I was not with my husband when your men asked for supplies. My husband, Nabal, is foolish, as his name suggests; he is always acting unwisely. The Lord has sent me to stop you from avenging yourself, for by destroying my husband and household, you will spill the blood of innocent people and have that on your hands. Please accept these gifts and find it within yourself to overlook this offence that has been committed against you.'

It was not enough—I could see that it was not enough. What more could I say? Then the words seemed to spring up from within me.

'You fight the Lord's battles and I recognise he will give you a great kingdom. Even if your life is hunted, God will protect you; you will be held securely by the living God. But God will hurl your enemies away, like a stone being shot from a sling. If you show us mercy now, when you are leader of Israel, and God has done for you all that he has promised, you will not have needless bloodshed on your conscience, nor the burden of having avenged yourself. When the Lord has given you all of this, do not forget that I am your servant; remember me.'

With these words, I dared to look up. David scrutinised me and I could see admiration in his eyes; was it for my beauty or for my courage?

'Praise be to God: he sent you to meet me today,' he replied. 'You are full of wise words and good judgement. You have kept me from avenging myself and shedding blood. Were it not for you, the lives of many would have been lost this night. I accept what you have brought for me, so return in peace. I have granted your request.'

I left with an immense sense of relief, determined to tell Nabal all that had taken place. It was late by the time we got back, and a sheep-shearing feast fit for a king was in full swing. In the middle of it all was Nabal, drunk and rowdy, eating and making merry, celebrating without a thought for David's good men who had helped us, but to whom he was prepared to give nothing. There was absolutely no point in speaking to him that night.

The next morning when Nabal was subdued after the feasting and drinking, I told him of the calamity that had nearly befallen us. My husband turned white, put his hand to his chest and keeled over, unable to move. I called the servants and Nabal was lifted to his bed, but he never recovered. Finally, ten days later, the Lord took his life.

Not long afterwards, a messenger sent by David himself arrived at my house asking to speak to me. David had been praising God for avenging Nabal's wrongdoing. He was grateful that, as a result of my words, he had been prevented from retaliation. Moreover, David requested that I become his wife!

How I hoped that David wanted me not only for my beauty, but also for my wisdom. How I hoped that he would love me. Had he not shown me respect and gratitude? Here was a man I could look up to: a man of proven integrity and valour, a man who loved God. I could love such a man. Besides, marrying David was certainly the most sensible action that I could take, giving me security and hope for the future, perhaps even bringing me happiness. Bowing to the ground, I responded,

'I am ready to do all my lord should want, even to wash the feet of his servants.'

I went immediately with the messenger, taking a donkey and my five women in attendance, stepping into my new life without a backward glance, determined to extend David's influence and family.

Reflection and discussion

- Did any words or phrases stand out for you?

- Abigail was a shrewd woman, managing her household well in difficult circumstances, committed to her responsibilities and working for peace. We see in her many of the attributes of the 'wife of noble character', described in Proverbs 31: 'She is clothed with strength and dignity' (v. 25), 'When she speaks her words are wise' (v. 26), 'She carefully watches everything in her household' (v. 27). How can we develop Abigail's qualities?

- Abigail behaved honourably and courageously, even when her husband was behaving badly. Have you ever found yourself surrounded by those who are not acting with integrity? How did you deal with the situation? How are the qualities of courage and honour—knowing and doing what is morally right—linked? Do we remember to pray for these attributes?

- Abigail spoke diplomatically and with great wisdom; she approached David with humility and meekly asked for forgiveness, seeking a peaceful solution that would save her household and would leave David without the guilt of having shed innocent blood. She used her beauty, charm and wealth, as well as her words, to achieve this. We can offer all that we are and all that we have to God in our service to him and others. Share times when you have been able to use who you are or what you have to serve God, perhaps in surprising ways.

- Like Abigail, our words can have a positive influence on others. We read in Proverbs, 'The words of the wise bring healing' (12:18), 'The wise are known for their understanding, and pleasant words are persuasive' (16:21), 'Kind words are like honey—sweet to the soul and healthy for the body' (16:24), 'Wise words are like deep waters; wisdom flows from the wise like a bubbling brook' (18:4). Share times when someone's words have persuaded you to take a wise course of action. Take time to pray that your words will be beneficial to others.

- Read Proverbs 31:30–31. Abigail had charm and beauty, but of even more value, she feared the Lord, as we can see in her words to David in 1 Samuel 25:24–31. Abigail was rewarded for what she did: she received David's praise for both her wisdom and her good judgement; she gained a secure future and she married a man whom she could respect. Read 1 Peter 3:3–5. What do you consider to be 'the beauty that comes from within'?

- David and Abigail start their marriage with mutual respect and gratitude. How do these two qualities contribute to all successful relationships? How can we foster closeness in our relationships in a modern world characterised by busyness and technology?

Conclusion

Take time to pray through your findings. What might God be saying to you? Is anything particularly relevant to your life at the moment? Write down what you have learnt and refer back to it regularly in the days ahead so that it becomes part of your thinking, reacting and lifestyle.

Abigail (Part 2)

Introduction

- Read 1 Samuel 25:43–44; 27:1–6; 30:1–6, 16–20; 2 Samuel 2:2–4; 1 Chronicles 3:1.

- Ask God to speak to you through this episode. You could use the words from 2 Thessalonians 3:16: 'Now may the Lord of peace himself give you his peace at all times and in every situation. The Lord be with you all.'

- Sit back, relax and close your eyes. Imagine the scene as someone reads the monologue.

Monologue

David was determined to extend his territory; in order to have a strong household he believed he needed many sons. Therefore, he not only married me, but also Ahinoam of Jezreel.

My life with David could not have been more different from the one I had been accustomed to. My previous comfort and security were swapped for the necessity of keeping away from Saul, who was forever searching for David. Consequently, we were always on the move. When an opportunity arose for my husband to kill Saul, he refused, saying that Saul remained the Lord's anointed one.[1] David constantly sought peace; Saul had ample evidence that David meant him no harm. My admiration for David grew daily: what mercy he had shown Saul; what honour he gave to God; how well he led his men, having both their loyalty and their love.

David was realistic; he knew from past experience that Saul would not leave him alone forever and he therefore sought safety for us all—his men and household. There was one place he believed Saul would never follow us: Philistia, beyond the borders of Israel. David spoke with Achish, king of Gath, and we were given Ziklag as a place of refuge. This was our home for a year and four months. All the time, David learned from the military skills of the Philistine commanders. Shrewdly he built his wealth by attacking the enemies of Israel. All this time, Achish thought that David was attacking communities *within* Israel; therefore he believed that David would never be able to return to his own land, for he would be hated there. He considered David to be totally in his power.[2] So he came to trust my husband to the point of making David and his men the rear bodyguard when the Philistines went out to attack Israel. I could hazard a guess at my husband's next move.

Meanwhile, we were left in Ziklag with our children. However, not many days after their departure a cry went up that the Amalekites were attacking us. There was mayhem: screaming, crying, fire everywhere. We ran frantically from our homes and out of Ziklag as the flames leapt higher and higher. All the Amalekites had to do was to round us up from every side. Like a flock of sheep, we were led away from Ziklag. As I looked back over my shoulder, I wept. We had no hope—David and his men were far away.

We walked three days in the heat, given just enough food and drink to survive. Young children were carried, babies wept for lack of milk. Hatred for their captors festered in the hearts of those boys who were nearly men. Finally, it seemed we were to be allowed to rest awhile. Weak with exhaustion, we huddled in groups; children were rocked into fitful sleep; despair gnawed at our hearts. Meanwhile, our captors ate, drank and danced in celebration of their success in capturing us and taking so much plunder.

As twilight fell, I thought I could see movement in the distance, shadows moving stealthily forwards. Suddenly, seemingly out of nowhere, men were charging into the camp, swords flying. Our captors, taken completely by surprise, were slow to put hands to their weapons. First our guards were killed lest they turned on us; it seemed that some of our rescuers had been assigned to surround and protect us. Then I saw him: David brandishing his sword with courage and shouting directions to his men. The slaughter continued; some of our captors took an opportune moment to escape on camels. Still the fighting went on, all the next day until once again daylight faded and not one Amalekite was left standing. It was then that David approached the throng of women and children, calling for us. The shouts of other men could then be heard as each called for his wife and family.

David was able to return us all safely to Ziklag with not only our goods intact, but also with the wealth that the Amalekites had gained from their other battles. I learnt from David that he and his men had returned early to Ziklag because some of the Philistine commanders had not trusted David to fight alongside them.[3] But for this circumstance, David would not have known what had befallen us and would not have rescued us. I shuddered at the thought.

Not long afterwards, news reached us that saddened my husband deeply: Israel was defeated by the Philistines; Saul and Jonathan were among the dead.[4] David had maintained a loyalty to Saul, and I saw now the depths of the extraordinary friendship that he had shared with Jonathan. I knew he had revealed the secrets of his heart to Jonathan in a way that he had not and would not with any of his wives. There was little that I could do to comfort him as I heard his lament and watched him grieve: 'Jonathan lies slain on your high places. I am distressed for you, my brother Jonathan; very pleasant have you been to me; your love to me was extraordinary, surpassing the love of women.'[5]

I sensed a change in David; he seemed to know that he was at a crossroads and spent much time in prayer. Then came the day when he shared his plans: we were all to go to Hebron in Judea, both his household and all his followers. Hebron was the highest point, and therefore of great importance and significance to our people. It was the place where Abraham, Sarah, Isaac, Rebecca, Jacob and Leah were buried. David was making a statement. As the largest city in Judea, it was well-fortified. Having a central location in the middle of trade routes, it was a good place to receive supplies, an ideal place for David to establish himself.

Hebron was known as a city of refuge and it became a city of refuge for us all. After our arrival, the leaders of Judah came and anointed David as king. Our wanderings were over. Once the wife of a scoundrel, I was now a wife of the king.

However, we were to live through seven further years of turmoil. By the time we arrived in Hebron, Saul had only one surviving son, Ish-bosheth,[6] who had been made king of Israel. David was often away fighting; slowly but surely the house of David became stronger and the house of Saul weaker.[7] David took more wives in order to strengthen his position with neighbouring areas and to be sure of future heirs. The price that I paid for royalty and security was rivalry and jealousy. Within seven years of arriving at Hebron, David had six sons.

Ahimoam gave birth to Amnon; I had a son, Daniel; Absolom was born to Maacah; Adonijah to Haggith; Shehatiah to Abital and Ithream to Eglah. Those sons grew up in an atmosphere that bred hostility.

Eventually the defeat of Ish-bosheth came from within his own army: he was slain by two of his captains. David was dismayed, for he believed vengeance should come from the hand of the Lord.[8]

The Israelites came to David at Hebron, requesting his leadership. From then on my husband was king not only of Judah, but also of Israel.[9] It was only a matter of time before David took Jerusalem and we all moved to live there. David took yet more wives and concubines; his family as well as his kingdom grew.[10] The tensions among us also multiplied. I could only watch as the troubles within his family brought David unending sorrow.

Footnote

It is likely that Abigail's son Daniel died young as he is not referred to again; the order of David's heirs was Amnon, then Absolom and next Adonijah.

Reflection and discussion

- Did any words or phrases stand out for you?

- David seemingly built up the strength of his household through his marriages. However, it appears that this was very much the 'world's' way of doing things, for it was so far from the early commands God gave to his people. We see the results—the jealousies, bitterness, betrayals, and other repercussions—of David's choices and actions. His family life was full of heartbreak and often split his kingdom rather than strengthening it. It is easy to follow the 'norms' around us and become so used to them that we accept them, even live by them. What seems like the easy or obvious way out can eventually harm us and those we love if it is not in accord with God's ways for us to live. Can you see examples of this in your own life, in your wider circle and society, and further afield in world events? How can we guard against this?

- Abigail must have needed courage to face the circumstances that came her way. Her life with David was initially insecure. She lived with the vulnerability of knowing they were being hunted down by Saul and then dwelt in the hostile territory of the Philistines. Share times when you have lived with insecurity and vulnerability, even hostility. How did God strengthen you to endure? How did these circumstances cause you to grow mentally and spiritually? Read Romans 8:28.

- An aspect of courage seems to be the ability to be flexible. Flexibility enabled Abigail to be resilient, as she underwent many changes in lifestyle. We read that the apostle Paul learned 'the secret of being content in any and every situation, whether well fed or hungry, whether living in plenty or in want' (Philippians 4:12, NIV). We may not face such extremes, but our inner well-being is still dependent on our flexibility, as our lives inevitably bring welcome and unwelcome changes. How are you getting on in the journey to become 'content'? Share your thoughts, particularly what has helped you to become more content.

- Ziklag and Hebron were places that offered Abigail some temporary respite, places where she could settle and put down some roots for a while. God often blesses us in this way but ultimately wants us to find our 'dwelling place' in him. Read Psalm 90:1, Ezekiel 37:27 and Jesus' words in John 14:23. Share times when you have been challenged to find your security, your 'dwelling place', in the Lord rather than in a physical place.

- The attack and abduction must have been terrifying for Abigail and the other inhabitants of Ziklag. Read Psalm 46:1–3. If you are able, share times when you have been in alarming circumstances and how God was your 'refuge and strength'.

- Abigail's safety and rescue came from unexpected quarters: the rejection of David and his men by some of the Philistine commanders. Without this, they would not have returned to Ziklag in time to save their families. Have there been times in your life when a rejection has had a greater purpose than was apparent at the time. When has help come to you from 'unexpected quarters'?

- Women and children are often the innocent victims in war. Many are traumatised by what they have seen and experienced. Many have been abducted. Who are in this position at the moment throughout our world? Take time to pray for those who come to mind.

- In the monologue Abigail commented on the hostility and trouble within David's family. Much of this stemmed from the hard-heart attitudes of covetousness and jealousy. What are we promised in Ezekiel 36:26–27? How can we combine being 'strong and courageous' (Joshua 1:6) with having a 'tender, responsive heart?' (Ezekiel 36:26)

Conclusion

Take time to pray through your findings. What might God be saying to you? Is anything particularly relevant to your life at the moment? Write down what you have learnt and refer back to it regularly in the days ahead so that it becomes part of your thinking, reacting and lifestyle.

The queen of Sheba

Introduction

- Read 1 Kings 10:1–13. (The narrative is also recorded in 2 Chronicles 9:1–12.)

- Ask God to speak to you through this episode. You could use the words from 1 Kings 3:9: 'Give me an understanding heart so that I can… know the difference between right and wrong.'

- Sit back, relax and close your eyes. Imagine the scene as someone reads the monologue.

Monologue

My land, Sheba, is a rich country, plentiful in gold, spices and precious stones. My people trade in these luxury goods far and wide. I had always taken great pride in my kingdom. Nevertheless, I knew that my wealth did not compare with that of the king of Israel, Solomon. His increasing power and riches seemed to know no bounds. His large fleet now travelled down the Red Sea to Ophir. The sailors told not only of his great wealth, but also of his outstanding wisdom.[1] The man intrigued me—what was the secret of his success and who was this God he worshipped who had supposedly made him so wise? He seemed too good to be true—perhaps there were hidden flaws within him: weaknesses, gaps in his knowledge and wisdom, waiting to be discovered. The more I heard, the more my curiosity grew and my envy was inflamed. He seemed to manage his people so well, resolving their disputes, enjoying peace and popularity. I knew the anxiety and demands of being queen: making the final decisions; listening to the advice of a never-ending stream of officials; seeking to make the best choices for my people. It was a lonely role; I wished to meet the man who seemed to do all this with such ease, such dignity and such success. Perhaps such a meeting would also develop the trade links between us, I reasoned. My restlessness was accompanied by a deep dissatisfaction, a thirst that I longed to quench.

I made the decision: I would make the journey of 1500 miles north-west to Jerusalem where I would have an audience with this man. What lengthy preparations were made and what a tough journey it was—the seemingly endless miles across the desert along the spice trading route, the heat by day and the cold of night, the sandstorms, the sameness of it all. The caravan stretched as far as the human eye could see—camels loaded with spice, gold, precious stones. I was out to impress.

Solomon's welcome was warm, the hospitality remarkable, the towns and cities prosperous; the countryside thrived with crops, vines and olives and with green pastures for their flocks.[2] My first view of Jerusalem is engraved on my mind—the awesome beauty of the palace and temple. Solomon himself took me to see the temple and I admired the gold, the carvings, the precious stones, the grand pillars, the doors of olive wood and the bronze basins. The building of the temple, I was informed, had taken 20 years of labour, careful planning and commitment. The palace too was striking. Solomon told me of the 13 years of its construction using cedars from Lebanon, built on a stone foundation.[3] The windows, colonnades, porticos and pillars were majestic in their proportions. I saw the hall of the throne and the hall of justice where Solomon pronounced judgements. Every section of them, from floor to ceiling, was covered in cedar wood. Then there was his private palace and the palace that had been built for his Egyptian wife. There seemed to be something almost indestructible about this beautiful city.

Through his building projects Solomon had developed close liaisons with other kings, including King Hiram of Tyre. Through his marriage alliance he had attained a peaceful relationship with Egypt. He controlled the trade routes; he was at the centre of our world. Many kings sent their ambassadors to learn from Solomon's wisdom and maintain diplomatic relations.[4] I had come to see and hear for myself.

I will never forget the conversations that I had with Solomon. I quickly realised that my attempts to catch him out, to prove him less wise or witty than me through riddles and puzzles, would come to nothing. Once I had discarded my superficial questions designed to trip him up, I found myself asking deeper and more meaningful questions: how he dealt with complex problems, managed his servants, his people, his relationships with other kingdoms—and I asked him about his God. There was nothing that I could not talk to this man about, no question too hard, no problem too complex.

I tasted the sumptuous food, listened as Solomon interacted with his servants and advisors, noted how well dressed they were and how well provided for. Here was a man one would be glad to serve, not from duty and necessity, but from genuine loyalty and respect. Here was a man who thought beyond the wealth he had accrued for himself and his people, beyond the security and influence he had as the earth's foremost leader, to the deep questions of life—how to know 'shalom', how to be at peace with God, oneself and others. Here was a man I could admire.

I learned from him a perspective that kept him both humble and vigilant: 'History merely repeats itself. It has all been done before, nothing under the sun is truly new,'[5] he told me. 'We don't remember what happened in the past, and in future generations, no one will remember what we are doing now.'[6] He understood the restless and covetous heart of man, saying, 'No matter how much we see, we are never satisfied.'[7] He told me of a point of despair in his life when he had discovered that pleasure and his work projects were not enough, all he had achieved was meaningless. Yes, meaningless, 'a chasing after the wind', he called it. For deep within our hearts God has placed a desire for himself, for the eternal;[8] without him we cannot be truly satisfied. From this place of anguish, Solomon had discovered the joy of a life of simplicity—food, drink and satisfying work, the enjoyment of which are gifts from God. He explained, 'God gives wisdom, knowledge and joy to those who please him.'[9]

There was such beauty and such poetry in the way that he spoke of God's eternal purposes: 'For everything there is a season, a time for every activity under heaven. A time to be born and a time to die. A time to plant and a time to harvest.'[10] The peace of his company was a balm to my striving, stressed spirit.

Not only did he speak beautifully, Solomon also wrote beautifully on numerous subjects, particularly love and wisdom. When I asked him to summarise all that he had learnt from God and from his life experience, he said, 'Fear God and obey his commands, for this is everyone's duty. God will judge us for everything we do, including every secret thing, whether good or bad.'[11] So the externals were not enough, I mused. God looks at our hearts, our motivations and objectives. Solomon spoke often of the heart. 'Who can say, "I have made my heart pure, I am clean from my sin?"'[12] He talked of his own sins of thought, action and negligence that he could not remedy. He told me of his regular visits to the temple where he offered burnt offerings to God. An innocent animal was slaughtered for his sin; it took the punishment he deserved. God had instructed this so that his people could know that their sins were forgiven and that they could be free from the guilt that weighs down the heart; moreover, they could be in fellowship with God. My gods were distant, gods to fear and placate; Solomon's God was his friend, as he had been his father, David's, before him. He exhorted me not to forget his God, the Creator, but to honour him.[13]

Oh, I couldn't tell you all the wisdom that I learned from this man, or value the gifts that he so generously bestowed on me before my return to Sheba. He asked me what I would like to take back with me: what I really wanted was his peace, his wisdom, his success—his God. I publicly praised God—the Lord—who had placed Solomon on the throne of Israel, whose benefits were not just for Israel, but spilled over into the surrounding countries through Solomon's justice and righteousness. I told him how my time with him had exceeded all my expectations and hopes, how privileged were those who worked for him and lived in his kingdom. How I wished that I could stay in this environment. But my own duties and land beckoned me; so with a full and changed heart, I returned.

Reflection and discussion

- Did any words or phrases stand out for you?

- The queen of Sheba had the courage to admit her dissatisfaction and to do something specific and major about it. Perhaps the enormous journey was partly diplomatic, but it was clearly for personal reasons too. 'When the queen of Sheba heard about the fame of Solomon and his relation to the name of the Lord, she came to test him with hard questions' (1 Kings 10:1, NIV). Sometimes hard questions about our faith may seem antagonistic, as no doubt hers did initially. However, the wise answers given by Solomon enabled her to be more open in her search. Read Colossians 4:5. How do we follow this advice in practice?

- Perhaps you have some hard faith-related questions to ask. If you are able, share these. What action can you take to move forward in your understanding?

- The queen of Sheba also had the courage to be honest and open to new ideas, being willing to travel a long distance in the search for answers. Jesus commends her for this. Read his words in Matthew 12:42 (NIV). 'The queen of the south', a Gentile, went to Israel, saw evidence of God's power and blessing, responded to God's wisdom and opened her heart in praise. She saw and believed. On the other hand, the Pharisees had not responded to Jesus, who was far greater and wiser than Solomon. In spite of the miracles that they had witnessed, they still wanted further evidence, 'a miraculous sign' (Matthew 12:38). They had all the proof needed to believe that Jesus was the Messiah. Today we have the evidence of the Bible, the guarantee of the Holy Spirit and the witness of Christians who have gone before us. If hearts have become hardened, no miraculous sign, not even the resurrection itself will convince. In what ways are we like the Pharisees, wanting a miraculous sign, when all we need to do is search the depths of God's word through his Spirit, the Spirit of truth?

- We do not know the full extent of the change in heart of the queen of Sheba, but her words of acknowledgement and the depths of her understanding of God's plans for Israel indicate a belief in Yahweh, 'Praise be to the Lord your God, who has delighted in you and placed you on the throne of Israel. Because of the Lord's eternal love for Israel, he has made you king to maintain justice and righteousness' (1 Kings 10:9, NIV). The life of a monarch affects the well-being of national and international relations. How have we seen this in the Bible and in world history?

- The queen of Sheba caught a glimpse of the big picture—God's wider design. Share occasions when you have seen beyond your habitual perspective and have seen God's bigger plan. Read Ecclesiastes 3:1–14. Discuss ways in which we can keep a God-centred perspective.

- Solomon was a blessing to the queen of Sheba: his company uplifted, inspired and challenged her, changing her outlook. Think of people who do this for you. How do they accomplish this? How can we be those who bless others in this way? Read 1 Thessalonians 5:11.

- There are some marked similarities between the queen of Sheba and the magi (Matthew 2:1–12): they travelled far, bringing gifts for the king; they were Gentiles on a genuine search; they responded to the King of Kings in praise and worship; they returned home transformed by their experience. Share times when you have been on a course, conference, retreat or holiday that has been a landmark in your spiritual journey. How can we maintain change after 'highs' such as the queen of Sheba's visit to Solomon must have been?

- The queen of Sheba discovered that the God of the Israelites was a personal God who acts specifically in the lives of men: choosing Solomon as king, giving him gifts of wealth and wisdom, granting him success. The way Solomon treated others, whatever their social standing, stemmed from his personal relationship with God. Read 1 Kings 10:23–24. All benefited from his wisdom. How well do we know the wisdom literature: Proverbs, Ecclesiastes and Song of Solomon? These are such practical books and have much to teach us about wise living. Why not commit to reading them, sharing what you have learnt at your next meeting?

- The queen of Sheba also discovered that God delights in those who follow him, for she said to Solomon, 'Praise be to the Lord your God, who has delighted in you' (1 Kings 10:9, NIV). Solomon's other name, Jedidiah, means 'beloved by God' (2 Samuel 12:25). Have we discovered the delight God takes in us? Meditate on the words, 'The Lord's delight is in those who fear him, those who put their hope in his unfailing love' (Psalm 147:11).

- In the monologue, Solomon shared with the queen of Sheba some of the thoughts that he wrote down (found in the book of Ecclesiastes) regarding simplicity and his realisation that God is behind the everyday pleasures that we enjoy. What aspects of life did he say are to be treasured (Ecclesiastes 4:9; 5:18–20; 6:9)? Our lives tend towards hurry and complexity. What rebalances us?

- We can make the Christian life very complex; Solomon told the queen of Sheba what was really needed—to 'fear God' and to 'remember your Creator' (Ecclesiastes 12), who is the source of all wisdom. What does this mean? Look at what God says he requires of us in Micah 6:8 and in Luke 10:27–28.

Conclusion

Take time to pray through your findings. What might God be saying to you? Is anything particularly relevant to your life at the moment? Write down what you have learnt and refer back to it regularly in the days ahead so that it becomes part of your thinking, reacting and lifestyle.

The widow with two sons

Introduction

- Read 2 Kings 4:1–7.

- Ask God to speak to you through this episode. You could use the words from Habakkuk 3:2: 'I have heard all about you, Lord. I am filled with awe by your amazing works. In this time of our deep need, help us again as you did in years gone by.'

- Sit back, relax and close your eyes. Imagine the scene as someone reads the monologue.

Monologue

I could bear it no longer. My husband had been a good man, a member of the group of prophets who supported Elisha. The anger, bitterness and heartache seemed to fill me to a point where I could not but burst. I decided to go to Elisha. When I found him, my pent-up emotions overflowed. I shouted in his direction, little caring that heads were turning to look at me, for what did reputation matter when I had lost so much?

'My husband is dead. You know how he loved God and served you and yet look at us now! I have no way of paying my bills, so my creditor is going to take my two boys as slaves. Is that how your God rewards devotion? Without them I will have no reason to carry on.' My anger melted to despair and I leaned against the well for support.

Elisha came alongside me and said gently, in a voice filled with compassion, 'I wonder what I can do for you. What do you have?'

'I have nothing,' I said. 'Well, almost nothing. Just a tiny bit of oil.'

Elisha was quiet for a few moments, deep in thought, then, turning to me, he said with great seriousness, 'This is what you must do: get all the jars, jugs and bowls you can find, borrow from your friends and neighbours. Then take your boys inside and shut the door, and start pouring and fill the containers.'

With a withering look, I walked away. It was not the first time that I had thought that the prophet was mad. But as I went, a voice inside my head asked, 'What would your husband do?' This had been my guiding light since his death, trying to think what my husband would have done in each situation that came our way. I knew that he would have followed Elisha's instructions. I had little to lose, I mused, and perhaps something to gain.

It was not long before my boys tumbled into our home, handsome but thin, too thin. 'I want you to collect all the containers you can,' I told them. 'No questions now. You'll see why.'

As they shuffled out, looking puzzled and decidedly unenthusiastic about the task, I thanked God silently that they were obedient children. Soon they were racing in and out, pots of all shapes and sizes filled our floor… and still they brought more.

'People keep asking why you want them,' my eldest said.

'And what do you reply?' I asked tentatively.

'No idea!' he exclaimed. 'Why do we want them?'

'Shut the door!'

A silence fell as they turned back to look at me, the question hanging in the air. What if nothing happened? How could I risk shaking the little faith they had left in a God who cares?

I told them carefully and quietly about my meeting with Elisha and his instruction. 'So now all we have to do is pour.'

No one moved. We were rooted to the spot.

After what seemed an age, my youngest son whispered, 'Give me the oil!'

Then he looked around for a while and carefully chose the smallest pot. He stood by it, with an intense expression on his face. It was the very look that I used to see on his father's face. Then he poured and in a moment it was done—the tiny pot was brimming with olive oil! None of us spoke. His older brother took the oil from him and chose the largest pot. We stood mesmerised as the oil flowed from my tiny container into this urn.

'Your turn,' they said, looking at me.

I turned to the nearest pot; did *I* believe? They had sufficient faith, but did *I*? My faith was as small as the tiny amount of oil in my hand. But what I had, I used, and as I started to tip my wrist, the drops of oil flowed and flowed until they streamed from the tiny container.

So we poured and laughed and poured and laughed.

'Next jug,' I said yet again.

'That's it,' my sons replied, and we looked in my little container—not a drop of oil was there. My youngest son took it and shook it upside down; the oil had stopped flowing. Our laughter was replaced by silent wonder.

'Stay there,' I instructed the boys, and ran back out to the well. There sat Elisha, still and silent, and there he remained while I excitedly told him what had taken place.

He smiled and said, 'All you have to do is sell the oil and pay your debts. With the money left over, you and your sons can live, love and rejoice in God's provision.'

So we did just that and my boys grew to have the measure of faith that only such an experience of utter dependence on God can give. Their father would have been so proud of them.

Reflection and discussion

- Did any words or phrases stand out for you?

- The prophet was a mediator between the people and God. He heard from God and passed on God's message to the people; they often approached God through the prophet. Christ is the mediator between us and God. Read 1 Timothy 2:5. What do you understand by this?

- We can come as honestly to God as this woman did to the prophet Elisha. Like the psalmist, we can pour out our hearts to God. What would you say to God about your life? Are there disappointments, anger, bitterness or resentments? If you are able, share these and pray for one another, placing these things at the cross, for Jesus bore our sorrows and sufferings so that we can live freely. Take time in the days ahead to meditate on Isaiah 53.

- This woman carried a huge weight of responsibility for these two boys. We may be burdened with a load of responsibilities for family members or in other areas of life. Share these and commit to supporting and praying for one another. Read Galatians 6:2, Psalm 55:22 and 1 Peter 5:7. How do we 'cast' our 'cares on the

Lord'? Are there helpful, symbolic ways of doing this that reflect our inner decision not to 'carry the burden'?

- The woman faced the threat of separation from her children. Are there any women you know of who live with this pain? Pray for women throughout the world, who find themselves separated from their children.

- The prophet asked the woman what she possessed, focusing on the little she had and not on all that she had lost. How do you feel about this? Does it seem unjust in view of her overwhelmingly difficult circumstances? Do you naturally look at life as half-full or half-empty? Do you tend to see the opportunities around you or the limitations of your circumstances? Share your thoughts. Read Romans 12:2. What attitudes and habitual thought patterns would you like to change?

- The woman did not receive an easy answer from Elisha or a handout, but was given words of promise. However, this promise depended on her having sufficient courage to take action. If she had not been able to grasp that thread of hope and follow Elisha's instructions, she would have missed out on the miracle. She had to cooperate with God in order to move forwards. How does this equate to your life at the moment? Fear and anxiety can immobilise us. Are there areas where you need the courage to take action?

- The woman in the monologue had to do two things that took courage: firstly, she had to trust and give responsibility to others (in her case, her children); secondly, following the prophet's instruction required her to ask for help from others. Do we find it hard or easy to delegate and to trust others, especially those with less experience? Is it easier to give than to receive? Do we possess the humility to receive from others, even to receive God's provision from the hands of others? Read 1 Corinthians 12:18–21. How can self-sufficiency be a barrier between us and our relationships with others?

- In the monologue, the woman was concerned about protecting her children's faith in a God who cares. Seeing authentic lives (faith applied and lived out in our everyday situations) is said to be the most powerful factor in encouraging our children to continue in their own faith journeys. Is there any faith-filled project you could become involved with as a family or with a group of believers, such as sponsoring a child, or an environmental project? Are there opportunities ahead in your life that will develop your faith and be life-changing for you and those close to you?

- In the monologue, the children were the first to pour the oil. We are told in the Bible that we need to become like children in the simplicity, sincerity and humility of our faith. Read Matthew 18:3. Are there times when you have learnt from or been strengthened by the faith of a child?

- Joy is a sustainer—'the joy of the Lord is your strength' (Nehemiah 8:10). The widow journeyed from hopelessness to joy. How much joy and celebration do you experience in your life? Ask for God's outpouring of joy, a fruit of the Spirit (Galatians 5:22) as you come to know him more as Jehovah Yireh, the God who will provide (Genesis 22:14), both in the small details of your life and the large concerns. Are there areas of your life that you could trust to God's provision? Share these and pray for one another.

Conclusion

Take time to pray through your findings. What might God be saying to you? Is anything particularly relevant to your life at the moment? Write down what you have learnt and refer back to it regularly in the days ahead so that it becomes part of your thinking, reacting and lifestyle.

The woman from Shunem (Part 1)

Introduction

- Read 2 Kings 4:8–37.

- Ask God to speak to you through this episode. You could use the words from 2 Peter 3:18: 'But grow in the grace and knowledge of our Lord and Saviour Jesus Christ. To him be glory both now and for ever! Amen' (NIV).

- Sit back, relax and close your eyes. Imagine the scene as someone reads the monologue.

Monologue

Shunem, a town on the fruitful Plain of Jezreel, had been a place of blessing for us. My husband's land flourished and we enjoyed wealth, status and security. He and I were respected throughout the town. My life was full: running the household; increasing our wealth through wise purchases and investment; caring for the poor and any who came my way who were in need.[1] My husband, many years older than me, loved, trusted and respected me. I thanked the God of our forefathers for his goodness to us, taking nothing for granted. However, few of us have everything we want in life and I lacked one thing which no amount of activity or fulfilment could replace. I longed for a child.

God had brought into our lives a holy man, the prophet Elisha, who often travelled through Shunem. I had pressed him to join us for a meal the first time he had come to our town. That day was the start of a friendship which blossomed with each of his visits. I sensed that he needed more than good food and conversation—he needed a refuge, a place where he could be alone with God. I saw his love for God, his deep commitment to God's laws and the way in which he gave of himself to all around him, but I could also see his exhaustion. The more I spoke to him, the more I realised the extent of the burdens that he carried on his shoulders.

'Why don't we adapt the roof space and build a small room in it, furnishing it with a bed, chair, table and lamp?' I asked my husband. 'Then, when Elisha comes here, he can stay with us and rest in peace and quiet.'

My husband readily agreed, so I set about the organisation of this project, anticipating with pleasure the moment when Elisa would see his room. Needless to say, he was delighted with it. On one visit, Elisha was in need of a rest, so he decided to take advantage of his retreat and sleep awhile.

Busy as I was, I hardly noticed the hours go by. In deep thought, I was interrupted by Elisaha's servant, Gehazi. I had not heard him enter the room.

'Elisha would like me to take you to speak to him,' he said.

Surprised, I followed Gehazi up to Elisha's room.

'You have done so much for me. How can I help you?' I was asked. 'I have influence with the king and the commander of the army—I can speak on your behalf to bring you some benefit.'

'Thank you, but I am happy here among my people and we have all we need,' I answered.

As I returned downstairs, I heard Elisha say to his servant, 'There must be something we can do for her.'

Continuing my work, I rejoiced in knowing that what we had done for Elisha had meant so much to him and had made such a difference in his life. I appreciated his gratitude and his affirmation. But after a few minutes, Gehazi called my name, asking me to return upstairs. Once again I stood in the doorway, waiting for Elisha to speak.

'At this time next year you will be holding a son,' he announced.

'Oh man of God, do not say things that cannot be, will never be,' I replied in anguish.

But soon there was no doubt that I was pregnant and the following spring I nursed my darling son. He became a delight to Elisha as well as to us.

Our son was the joy of my husband's heart. It was a mutual adoration. My son loved nothing better than to be in his father's company and, as soon as he was able, followed him everywhere. Our son was safe with our reapers and would often choose to be outside with them, a shadow at his father's heels.

The day had started like any other; our son was out in the fields with his father. But just a couple of hours later, my husband's servant hurried into the house carrying the boy.

'What's happened?' I asked.

'He complained to his father of a headache. It seemed to come on very quickly and, seeing that he was so unwell, I was asked to bring him to you,' the servant replied.

My first thoughts were that the sun had been too strong and, as I sat with my child on my lap, I ordered water to be brought to us. There we remained, his head on my shoulder. Initially he took a little water, but all too rapidly he started to lose consciousness. With a rising panic I bathed his face and body with cool water, attempting to reduce his fever, but to no avail. I sang to him, rocked him, whispered gently to him, but he did not even open his eyes. His breathing became strained, then shallow and I knew that I was losing him. As the sun rose to the highest point in the sky, he breathed his last.

I could have wailed and screamed, revealing our terrible loss, but instead in deep shock I carried my dear boy and gently laid him on Elisha's bed, shutting the door. After that, I gave instructions to the servants to leave my child undisturbed and went out to find my husband. As soon as I saw him I called out, 'Send one of the servants with a donkey. I must go and see Elisha.'

'Why now?' my husband replied with surprise. 'It's not a holy day, the new moon or Sabbath.'

'I know. I'll be back quickly. All is well,' I told him.

I saddled the donkey myself and set off with one of our servants, urging him to go as quickly as he could. We headed for Mount Carmel, 20 miles from our small town, for that was where I knew I would find Elisha. It was a place where God had revealed himself in power to the prophet Elijah,[2] a place of great significance to Elisha.

I saw a figure running towards us and soon recognised him as Gehazi.

'Is everything all right with you, your husband and child?' he shouted.

'All is well,' I replied.

As soon as we came to the man of God, I fell at his feet and held on to him, unable to utter a word. Gehazi, no doubt taken aback by my loss of dignity, attempted to pull me away. But Elisha stopped him. Through my moans and tears, I heard his voice, calm but deeply concerned, 'Leave her! She is in deep distress. The reason for her grief is hidden from me; God has not yet disclosed it to me.'

I could not say the words 'my son has died'. The words that I *could* utter were accusatory and angry: 'Did I ever ask you for a son? No! Didn't I even say "don't deceive me" when you said that I would have one?'

If I had never had a son and never known what it was to love another so unconditionally, I would not have had to experience such unspeakable sorrow or bear such a crushing blow. This man of God had brought me pain. I looked into his eyes and knew that now he realised what had happened: God had revealed to him my plight. Straight away, Elisha handed his staff to Gehazi, instructing him to run to Shunem, stopping for no one, and to lay his staff on my boy's face.

I dared to hope. 'As surely as God lives, I won't leave you; I won't go home without you,' I said to Elisha. Filled with compassion, Elisha agreed to come back with me.

As we neared Shunem, we saw Gehazi running towards us. My hope soared, only to fade when I saw his facial expression. 'He hasn't woken up,' he said.

In silence we returned to the house and climbed the stairs; in silence we looked at my child's lifeless form. Elisha asked us to leave him alone with my son.

I stood at the foot of the steps waiting, every moment seeming like an eternity. There was not a sound. Then I heard Elisha's footsteps pacing back and forth overhead; next, all was quiet once again. I could bear the tension no longer and stumbled outside, seeking solace in the late afternoon scent of herbs, barely able to see where I was going through my tears.

Then I heard it, coming from the upstairs window: the sound of a sneeze, then another and another—seven sneezes! A woman knows not only the sound of her child's cry and his laugh, but also the sound of his sneeze. The first sneeze I could have imagined; the second one convinced me that I was not dreaming. I stood still, listening, hope rising within me. Turning, I saw Gehazi, his arms raised, his face joyful, calling me to come quickly. I hurried to the room and there was my son, his eyes wide open, his face pale, looking bewildered. I fell at Elisha's feet bowing down low, but Elisha drew me up.

'Pick up your son,' he said.

How tenderly I drew him into my arms, cradled him close to my heart and carried him downstairs, leaving the prophet to commune with the Lord.

Reflection and discussion

- Did any words or phrases stand out for you?

- The Shunammite woman 'practised hospitality' (Romans 12:13). She spotted Elisha's needs for food, shelter, rest, space and privacy. Are there people you know in need of any of these? Perhaps you feel in need of them yourself. Share your thoughts.

- She understood that, although a great prophet, Elisha, too, was a mortal who could feel spent and be in need of support. What does this teach us about how we should treat our spiritual leaders and others who give so much of themselves? Read Galatians 6:9–10 and Hebrews 13:7, 17. It seems that in caring for our leaders, we care for ourselves. This was certainly true for the Shunammite woman. How could it be true for us?

- The story speaks to us of simplicity. The woman from Shunem provided a small room with a bed, table, chair and lamp; this is what Elisha needed. We often confuse our wants with our needs, which can lead to covetousness and contribute to both a lack of contentment and an unhelpful drive to earn and possess. How can we distinguish our wants from our needs? Simplicity is regarded by many as a spiritual discipline that enables us to live more freely. How can we experience more simplicity in our lifestyles? In what ways have you simplified your life? Are there aspects that you would like to simplify? Are there ways in which you have or could declutter your life materially, mentally, emotionally or spiritually? In the weeks ahead, take some time out to act on this. Read Paul's advice in 1 Timothy 6:6–11.

- The woman from Shunem and her husband had the wealth to promote Elisha's well-being and were generous with what they owned. If we are blessed materially, we are in a position to share and bless others. There are many examples of this in the Bible: this woman provided a furnished room; women helped financially to support Jesus' ministry (Luke 8:3); Joseph provided his tomb (Luke 23:50–53); the believers shared their possessions (Acts 4:32). Can you think of other examples? We can be generous not only materially but also in the way we think about others and behave towards them. Read Proverbs 19:11, Luke 6:35–36 and Galatians 5:16, 22–23. How can we become more 'generous in spirit'?

- The woman from Shunem knew the joy of bearing a son and watching him grow, only then to experience his sudden death. The trauma of this tragedy must have been great and her emotional pain severe. Her courage enabled her to think clearly and carry out a quickly formed plan—to go to the man of God. She remained calm and maintained her dignity until she was with Elisha. If you are able, share times when God has given you a courage that has empowered you to remain calm and act with strength and dignity in difficult circumstances.

- The woman said twice that 'all is well' (2 Kings 4:23 and 26, ESV). What do you make of this? Do you think she is lying? If so, why? Or is she in a state of profound shock? Or is her faith of such depth and her courage so great that, in spite of her circumstances, she does believe that ultimately God is in control and therefore 'all is well'?

- When trouble came, the Shunammite woman turned to God by means of his prophet. Is it our first reaction to turn to God when trouble comes our way? The support of other believers can be of enormous help. Read Psalm 46:1–3, 10 and Galatians 6:2.

- Although her courageous faith in God took her to Elisha, this woman still experienced deep anguish, questioning God's dealings with her (2 Kings 4:28). We learn from her that courage may go hand in hand with distraught yet honest questions when we approach God. If you feel able, share times when this has been true for you. Have there been occasions when being honest about how you are feeling has been hard? Why? Honesty and transparency may take courage, but what are the benefits?

- In the monologue, the woman said, 'If I had never had a son and never known what it was to love another so unconditionally, I would not have had to experience such unspeakable sorrow or bear such a crushing blow.' We often experience pain in loving. This is evident in Jesus' story of the prodigal son (Luke 15:11–32). This parable shows the depth of God's compassion for us. The God who 'gave his one and only Son' (John 3:16) understands grief. His Son 'carried our sorrows' (Isaiah 53:4, NIV). When and how have you experienced God's loving compassion?

- The woman from Shunem showed courage in her assertive response, saying that she would not go home unless Elisha himself accompanied her. We are not to be intimidated by fear of what others may think, but neither are we to speak aggressively, but with respect (1 Peter 2:17). Paul told Timothy, 'For God has not given us a spirit of fear and timidity, but of power, love, and self-discipline' (2 Timothy 1:7). Pray for these qualities to grow within you. Are there areas of life where you need to be more assertive?

- The narrative ended joyfully with the young boy receiving back his life. However, he did not come back to life immediately. Why do you think this was the case?

- The Shunammite woman was 'overwhelmed with gratitude' (2 Kings 4:37). When was the last time that you experienced the joy of gratitude? How can we intentionally become grateful people?

Conclusion

Take time to pray through your findings. What might God be saying to you? Is anything particularly relevant to your life at the moment? Write down what you have learnt and refer back to it regularly in the days ahead so that it becomes part of your thinking, reacting and lifestyle.

The woman from Shunem (Part 2)

Introduction

- Read 2 Kings 8:1-6.

- Ask God to speak to you through this episode. You could use the words from Hebrews 1:8-9 and 12: 'Your throne, O God, endures forever and ever. You rule with a sceptre of justice. You love justice and hate evil... you are always the same; you will live forever.'

- Sit back, relax and close your eyes. Imagine the scene as someone reads the monologue.

Monologue

Elisha, God's holy prophet, was to shape our lives further. When he prophesied that there would be a drought in Shunem which would last for seven years, we had no doubt that this would come to pass. On this particular visit, Elisha not only prophesied the coming drought, but also warned us that we should leave before trouble struck. He did not say *where* we should go: that decision was left to us.

So at the end of a beautiful harvest, at the peak of our success and happiness, we were to be found packing up our belongings and taking our son away from all that he had known and loved. To those around us we must have seemed as mad as Noah building an ark when there was no sign of rain. What were we doing, leaving a land of plenty, flowing with milk and honey?

We moved to the land of the Philistines near the Great Sea, and there we spent seven years living in an alien culture, holding on to the faith of our forefathers. We heard much of the severe famine in Israel where crops failed year after year. I counted off the seven harvests, grateful that at least there was enough food for us in the house, but longing to return.

It was a time of great personal sadness, for my elderly husband, already frail when we departed Shunem, did not live to see his land again. My son was a great comfort to me and my hope for the future.

When, finally, the seven years of famine prophesied by Elisha were over, my household prepared to return to Israel. I filled the long hours of the journey by telling my son more of the home and land that would be his. I imagined how it would become fruitful once more, remembering its beauty. We found Shunem depressed after the years of poverty, a mere shadow of the place I had known. Moreover, to my dismay, our home and fields were not empty as I had expected, and the farmer who had taken them over was in no hurry to give them back. They were rightfully my son's possession and there was nothing for it but to appeal to the king. How I wished my husband was there to carry out this business!

I prayed for strength, dignity and favour with the king, for I knew that the outcome of this meeting would affect not only my son's life, but that of our whole household, for whom I was responsible.

Imagine my joy when, as my son and I were brought before the king, who should be talking to him but Elisha's servant, Gehazi! What was their topic of conversation?—the miracles that God had performed through Elisha. As we approached, Gehazi uttered in astonishment, 'Why, this is the very woman I have been speaking about, and this is her son whom Elisha raised from the dead!'

God had gone ahead of us preparing the way, placing Gehazi there to support me and to speak for me. The king asked me to verify Gehazi's story and I told him that it was indeed true. This opportunity enabled me to tell the king of my plight; we had obeyed Elisha's instruction to leave Israel, but now I desired to return to our home and pass on the land to my son.

Immediately the king appointed one of his officials to act on our behalf. We were to be granted even more than I had hoped for: not only was our land and home to be returned to us, but also the profit gained from the fields during the last seven years! Although this was limited because of the severity of the famine, it was enough to get us started again with seed for the fields. It gave us a future; praise be to God who provides and restores.

Reflection and discussion

- Did any words or phrases stand out for you?

- The woman from Shunem had a deep trust in the prophet Elisha and in his ability to discern God's will. Read 2 Peter 1:20–21. We are told in 1 Corinthians 14:1–4 to 'eagerly desire... the gift of prophecy' because it speaks to us for our 'strengthening, encouragement and comfort' (NIV). What do you understand from these words? We are warned that if we 'have the gift of prophecy... but have not love', we gain nothing (1 Corinthians 13:2–3, NIV). Why is this so?

- Although Elisha told the woman and her family to leave, they were not told where to go. This decision they had to make for themselves. Have you known times when God has pointed you in a certain direction in a general way, but you have had to use your God-given common sense to make decisions about the specifics? Share your experiences.

- The Shunammite woman courageously followed God when her action seemed foolish to those around her, and left for Philistia before there was a sign of famine. In our Christian lives we are often 'going against the flow', doing what is foolish in the world's eyes. Can you give examples, particularly from your own life? Read 1 Corinthians 1:24–29 and 2:12–14. What do you understand from these verses? Courage and humility go together—how?

- The seven years in the land of the Philistines must have seemed long to the woman of Shunem, developing her patience. Patience, a fruit of the Spirit (Galatians 5:22) is a virtue to be desired and to cultivate. How do we do this? Read James 5:7–8; Colossians 1:11 and 3:12–13. Share experiences that have or are teaching you to have patience. Perhaps you would like prayer for patience in a specific circumstance you are facing.

- No doubt the Shunammite woman went through the complexities of adapting to and living in a totally different culture, yet remaining true to the God of Israel. Are there people who have recently arrived in our communities? How could we contribute to making their transition easier?

- It must have taken courage for this woman to approach the king in order to ask for her rights to be met. She took action because she knew that her family had been wronged. Although the Bible requires us to be forgiving people, we are not asked to be passive, but instead to fight injustices on all levels. It can be easier to be assertive on behalf of someone else (as she was for the sake of her son) than for ourselves. Indeed, we are instructed to 'look not only to your own interests, but also to the interests of others' (Philippians 2:4, NIV). Think of practical ways in which you could fight for justice on behalf of those who cannot fight for themselves. You may wish to pray for the courage to tackle an unjust situation in your life.

- This story shows us the wonder of God's amazing timing, for when the woman of Shunem approached the king, Gehazi was there describing how Elisha brought a boy—her boy—back to life. What other moments of incredible timing can you recall from the Bible? How does this encourage us when the waiting seems long? Share instances of God's wonderful timing in your lives. Take time to meditate on Psalm 37:5-7.

- The presence of Gehazi gave the Shunammite woman support just when she needed it. He was part of God's provision for her. Share times when God has placed someone in your path to give you the very help or advice that you needed. Read Proverbs 27:9. Pray for the sensitivity to know when and how to give help or advice.

- The woman from Shunem lived with considerable ebbs and flows in her life. It takes courage and resilience to withstand change. Read Psalm 18:1-2 as well as Jesus' words in Matthew 7:24-25. How do these verses speak to you? This woman's past experience of God's goodness and faithfulness enabled her to endure the hardships that came her way and to work towards a hope-filled future. Like David we can say, 'Yet I am confident I will see the Lord's goodness while I am here in the land of the living' (Psalm 27:13).

- This narrative ends with restoration. Not all of our earthly difficulties will be resolved but we hold on to our final hope in God. Read Jeremiah 17:7-8. Share specific areas in your lives where you need more resilience. Pray for one another, that you will have not only the courage to survive, but will also thrive.

Conclusion

Take time to pray through your findings. What might God be saying to you? Is anything particularly relevant to your life at the moment? Write down what you have learnt and refer back to it regularly in the days ahead so that it becomes part of your thinking, reacting and lifestyle.

The young Jewish maid

Introduction

- Read 2 Kings 5:1–19.

- Ask God to speak to you through this episode. You could use the words from Philemon 6: 'I pray that you may be active in sharing your faith, so that you will have a full understanding of every good thing we have in Christ' (NIV).

- Sit back, relax and close your eyes. Imagine the scene as someone reads the monologue.

Monologue

I am hovering next to my mistress, watching my master, Naaman, as he stands before the altar that has been built from bricks made with the soil that he brought back from Israel. It is here that he now worships. Although he attends the temple of Rimmon with the king, providing an arm for the king to lean on, his bow to Rimmon is no more than a civic duty, so my mistress tells me. This must be true, for I can see the sincerity in his eyes as he worships the Lord God of Israel. I praise God with all my soul as I wait here with my mistress, sensing her joy and peace.

I could never have imagined such an answer to those frightened and desperate cries to God as I was dragged away from my family and friends. I remember the nightmares that disturbed my sleep when I first arrived in this household. Even in my slumber I could see the armed men breaking into my father's house, seizing objects and people to take as spoil, my mother's face, my screams, my father powerless to stand against them. My early days here were filled with an aching loneliness. The strangeness of their religion and customs isolated me. If I was not careful to guard my thoughts, they became filled with regrets for my lost freedom and the future that had been snatched from me—the woman I would not become, the man I would not marry, the way of life I would not lead, the home I would not run, the children I would not have. Better not to go there in my head, but to hold on to the words of one of the other captives: 'They have taken our bodies, but they cannot take our hearts, our faith, our God. His presence goes with us.'

The attack had come as a surprise, for Israel was not at war with Aram. However, my father and his friends did speak together of the threat from Aramean raids. They believed the raids were designed to intimidate us and demonstrate the growing power of the king of Aram. Since that time long ago when Aram had submitted to King David,[1] the peace between the countries had been precarious. The attack might have taken us by surprise, but it wasn't the first time they had raided and it would not be the last.

Exhausted after the long journey, we were taken to the Damascus market to be sold as slaves. I recall the heat and noise, the unfamiliar smells and words. Then the eyes of a man fixed on me. I dared not meet his gaze, but I could see from his attire and judge from the way others treated him that he was a man of the greatest importance. There seemed to be some bargaining going on and then I found myself being pulled out from the line of slaves. With a wave of his hand, the man indicated that I should follow him and his servants.

In that way I found myself in the household of Naaman, commander of the king's army, a great warrior and held in high esteem by the king. I was a present for his wife, a maid for her. I made it my concern to be as attentive to her requirements as I could. I was treated kindly, fed well, clothed as befitted my new role. My mistress, in spite of her position in society and my background, seemed to enjoy my presence and slowly a fondness grew between us. In a surprising way, I started to thrive, although my sense of loss was always there in the background. So was my faith; my prayers for my family started to be accompanied by prayers for my master and mistress. Gradually I learnt the language, the routines and, most importantly, how to please my mistress.

One day a change came over her. Quite suddenly her laughter departed and a sad nervousness took its place. I noticed that her husband no longer came to her at night, and yet her words regarding him were still full of care, her glances at him nevertheless tender. Her silence weighed heavily on me until I could bear it no longer. I dared to ask what was troubling her. What she told me shocked me greatly: Naaman had leprosy. It was so mild at that stage that they had told no one, but she knew it was only a matter of time before he would have to admit it, leave everything and everyone that he loved. Their future was in tatters and the situation seemed hopeless. But not to me. Unsure as to what her reaction would be, I told her about the prophet in Israel, a man named Elisha, who had received power from the God of Israel to perform miracles. Perhaps she saw my confidence and it gave her a shred of hope, for she repeated our conversation to her husband. Her hope sparked hope within him. Naaman dared to go to the king of Aram, spoke to him of his leprosy and the possibility that the prophet of Israel might be able to help him. With no time to lose, the king ordered gifts of gold, silver and clothing to be packed for Naaman to take to the king of Israel, along with a letter of introduction instructing Israel's king to heal my master of his leprosy.

Then we waited and waited; the house was filled with tension, the days dragged, the servants were in a constant state of readiness for his return. Finally, we heard news: Naaman was approaching. One look at his face was enough to tell us the wonderful news: he was well! How extraordinary—two of his mules were weighed down with baskets of earth! Naaman gave orders that this earth that he had brought back from Israel should be made into bricks straight away. I wondered what they were to be used for.

What rejoicing and celebrations the household experienced that day! My heart overflowed with gratitude to God who had demonstrated his healing power. Later my mistress repeated her husband's story to me. She spoke of the king of Israel's fear when asked to do the impossible—heal a man—for he believed that the king of Aram was looking for an excuse to start war. I listened intently as she told me that Elisha, hearing of the king's distress, had sent for Naaman. Yet when my master had arrived at his house, Elisha hadn't even come to the door, but had sent a messenger to him, instructing him to wash in the River Jordan seven times. The commander was furious at being treated like this, at being asked to perform such a mortifying action. He was above publicly washing in a foreign river. If he had wanted ritual cleansing, he would have washed in the superior rivers of Damascus, the Abana and the Pharpar. He was also deeply disappointed, for he had expected the prophet to cure him by waving his hand over the leprosy while he prayed to his God. Naaman's loyal officers, however, persuaded him to follow these simple instructions. My mistress's eyes sparkled with tears as she told me of the six unsuccessful dips in the river. I imagined his despair as, each time, he rose from the waters unchanged. Then she described his final step of obedience as he went down into the river for the seventh time, the joy of looking at his skin, perfectly clear, all signs of the white leprosy marks gone.

Naaman had returned to Elisha, who this time came out and spoke with him. My master had declared that he now believed in only one God, the God of Israel. The prophet would accept no gifts, but Naaman requested that he be allowed to take two sacks of earth so that he could worship God at an altar made from Israelite soil. My master was concerned that, once home, he would be required to accompany the king to the temple of Rimmon and bow with him. Would the Lord forgive Naaman? Elisha reassured him that God saw the heart[2] and that he should go in peace, for God was with him.

So, here I stand near the altar to my God, able to worship him in a foreign land. I am a valued member of a household where I have found love and been an instrument of restoration.

Reflection and discussion

- Did any words or phrases stand out for you?

- In the monologue, the young maid demonstrated courage in the way in which she accepted and lived with her circumstances. She kept her perspective and held on to her faith in God's love even though she had suffered greatly. Read Matthew 10:28–33. How do these words both challenge and comfort us?

- The maid chose to be hard-working, trustworthy and submissive, winning her mistress's respect. Even at her young age, she showed sympathy and care when she could have become withdrawn and bitter. Read Paul's instruction to the young Timothy in 1 Timothy 4:12. In what ways can we follow her example and Paul's recommendation? Are there areas in our lives where we need to pray for the courage to *choose* our responses?

- The young woman showed immense courage in speaking boldly to her mistress, telling her what God had done through the prophet Elisha. She did not excuse herself from the responsibility to speak out, either by thinking that she was too young or too insignificant, but instead was ready to share her faith in the God who had sustained her. Read Romans 5:3–5. Her suffering had led to perseverance, to the development of a strong character and finally to a hope that she could pass on to others when a crisis arose. Think of those you know who are downcast and pray for the opportunity to impart hope into their lives.

- The maid's actions had paved the way for her words. Read James 2:14–17. These are strong words, implying that speaking about our faith is both meaningless and hypocritical if our behaviour has not matched our words. Share examples of those whose behaviour and actions have inspired you to pay close attention to their words.

- A female slave, such as this maid, knew that her well-being depended totally on her mistress having a compassionate nature. Read Psalm 123:1–2 where the image of a maid and mistress is used to express our dependence on God's mercy and help. Our self-sufficiency is a fragile illusion, as Naaman had found out. Share times when you have been thrown into a reliance on God's grace and mercy, discovering the limits to your self-sufficiency.

- Although in a humble and restricted position, God had placed the maid where she was for a purpose. She was a crucial link in a chain that was to bring healing to Naaman and faith in the God of Israel to his household. Encourage one another by recounting situations when you have been a link in a chain where you perceive that God was at work.

- Problems are lessened when seen through the eyes of faith. The seemingly insurmountable difficulty faced by Naaman and his wife appeared so much smaller through the maid's eyes, for she believed that God could meet his need. Read Matthew 17:20 and Philippians 4:19. What do you understand from these verses?

- Pride nearly prevented Naaman from receiving the gift of healing—dipping in the River Jordan seven times was too humiliating an answer to his request for help. Pride often stands in our way—in the way of our relationships; in the way of making changes in our lives; in the way of turning to or responding to God; in the way of becoming more Christlike. Are there areas of your life where pride is holding you back? A humble attitude is not necessarily valued in today's society; therefore, it can take courage to choose to walk humbly with God instead of promoting oneself.

- Perhaps the answer was too simple for Naaman; maybe he wanted to buy his cure. He certainly expected Elisha to come out and 'perform' a miracle. The simplicity of the gospel, believing in Christ and receiving his forgiveness, can be an obstacle for people. Read John 3:16, Ephesians 2:8–10 and 1 Peter 2:24. Some would rather earn their salvation, instead of accepting it as a gift. Why do you think this is? Naaman's immersion in the River Jordan can be seen as a foreshadowing of baptism. Peter says in Acts 2:38, 'Each of you must repent of your sins and turn to God, and be baptised in the name of Jesus Christ for the forgiveness of sins. Then you will receive the Holy Spirit.' Naaman's decision to be humble led to him receiving both healing and faith. What do we receive through our faith in Christ—our 'spiritual blessings'? Look at Ephesians 1:1–14 to stimulate your thinking.

- God healed Naaman of leprosy. Today, some are healed miraculously and others live with ongoing pain and illness. How do you understand this?

- Naaman took some earth back to make bricks for an altar where he could sacrifice to God. We often want to hold on to experiences through reminders. This can be harmful if it prevents us from looking forward, but can be helpful if it encourages our faith and prompts us to remember God's grace in our lives. Some people are greatly helped by art, symbols, objects, places and memories that root their faith; others are not. Share your thoughts. We understand from Naaman's action that his healing had changed not just his body but his soul—he now wished to worship the God of Israel. It must have been a joyful moment for the maid when her master returned not only well but with faith in the living God, wanting his whole household to worship the God of Israel.

- Naaman was in a predicament, for he had a duty to perform (attending the temple of the god Rimmon with the king) that clashed with his new faith. He realised that worship of the one true God could not go alongside the worship of idols. There may be times when we have to attend or be part of events that are not in accord with our faith and values. Can you think of examples? How do we make such decisions?

Conclusion

Take time to pray through your findings. What might God be saying to you? Is anything particularly relevant to your life at the moment? Write down what you have learnt and refer back to it regularly in the days ahead so that it becomes part of your thinking, reacting and lifestyle.

Tabitha or Dorcas

Introduction

- Read Acts 9:36–42.

- Ask God to speak to you through this episode. You could use the words from 2 Corinthians 4:14: 'We know that God, who raised the Lord Jesus, will also raise us with Jesus and present us to himself.'

- Sit back, relax and close your eyes. Imagine the scene as someone reads the monologue.

Monologue

My name is Tabitha, which means 'gazelle', but like many Jewish people I am more often known by the Greek version of my name, Dorcas. I live in the coastal town of Joppa, a port with a natural harbour overlooking the Great Sea. The town is built around the waterfront and into the high cliffs surrounding it, and boasts a large Jewish population. Ten miles to the north-west of Joppa is Lydda, a thriving trading location built on the crossroads of the main route to Jerusalem and the route north to the coastal town of Caesarea, seat of the Roman government in Judea. Joppa itself is a centre for trade, fishing and the tanning of hides.

My life here had been financially comfortable until my husband died, and even then I quickly realised that, compared to many widows in the area, I was in a reasonable position money-wise. You see, I had a skill that I could trade: my sewing. The wealthier ladies liked clothes in shades of blue, made from linen and dyed with indigo or woad, or red, using dye from the madder plant and scarlet from the scale insect. For the poorer people I made clothes of undyed fabrics in cream, brown and black. I grieved greatly the death of my husband, but my occupation, keeping my hands busy with the methodical in and out of the needle, both absorbed my restless energy and gave me purpose. Later, as time passed, my sewing gave me my much-needed independence and sense of satisfaction. I was, however, to discover a far greater purpose.

News, as well as goods, travels along the road to Jerusalem and up and down the coastal routes. The Jewish people in Joppa had heard of the goings-on in Jerusalem and of the followers of the way.[1] We had even met some of them who had left Jerusalem for fear of being killed after witnessing the death of their friend, Stephen,[2] and experiencing a growing persecution there. Then one of their leaders,[3] Philip, arrived in Joppa. He had come from Azotos and was on his way up the coast, heading for Caesarea.[4] He had an amazing story to tell: how he had left Jerusalem and travelled to the city of Samaria, telling them about Jesus the Christ; how God had spoken to Philip and told him to go to the desert area on the road between Jerusalem and Gaza. There he had met an Ethiopian eunuch of great importance, a God-fearer, returning from worshipping God in Jerusalem, who was puzzling over the prophecies in Isaiah.[5] Philip had explained how the prophecies all pointed to the coming of Christ as the Messiah and had been fulfilled in the person of Jesus. Philip, we were to discover, had a gift for making the scriptures clear. The Ethiopian eunuch had become a follower of Jesus there and then and had been baptised.[6]

Immediately after the baptism, Philip had miraculously found himself at Azotus and, believing in God's guidance and direction, he continued telling people about Christ as he started to make his way up the coast. While he was with us, Philip explained the good news of how Christ had come to reconcile us to God, about his teaching, death and resurrection. As my heart responded to his words, I was changed. I became more deeply aware of the need around me.

There were many widows in Joppa: wives with young children who had lost their husbands to the stormy seas; older women who had outlived their husbands. The younger women needed help to clothe their families. The older ones often lacked the eyesight and dexterity to sew for themselves. I, in the middle of these age groups, had much to offer. I could buy fabrics and sew for them, clothe the old and young who had more difficulty than me in keeping warm in the cold winds that blew off the sea through our town. My sewing became a joy; my life regained a profound purpose. As I reached out to others, my own pain was lessened. I experienced a peace that was beyond understanding,[7] deeper even than my grief. It was as if what I was doing for these women, I was actually doing for Christ himself.[8] As I sewed, I nattered with these women, and a deep bond developed between us. Through our conversations, I discovered more ways in which they needed help with the everyday matters of life, and through the Holy Spirit, the Spirit of wisdom that we had witnessed in Philip,[9] I was able to respond.

That is, until the day when I woke with a burning headache. I was too ill to sew, and soon unable to eat, sit and talk. My fever rose; one minute I was hot and the next, desperately cold. I was vaguely aware of my friends fussing around me, mopping my brow and whispering to each other. Then I remember no more.

The first thing I was to become aware of was a man's voice. He seemed to be praying, calling me by my Aramaic name, Tabitha, and instructing me to get up. As I opened my eyes, I saw a stranger kneeling beside me, offering me a hand. I sat up slowly and shakily. In my weakness, I needed the strength of his hand to help me stand. Who was he, and why was he here? I felt as if I was coming out of the deepest of sleeps, the world around me seeming less real than the unseen world of my sleep. I realised that I was in my upper room, but how had I got there? Seeing my confusion, the stranger went quickly to the door and called in my friends. Why were they all in my house? Around the room I could see tunics and other garments that I had made. Why were they there? Some of the widows and believers entered the room and I could hear the man telling them that I was well. Then I remembered my headache. But why were their eyes so swollen, their faces tear-stained and strained? Why were they rushing in with exclamations of wonder and joy, taking me in their arms?

Slowly the story emerged; it was one that I would have found hard to believe but for their reactions and the presence of this man, whom I discovered to be none other than the apostle Peter, Jesus' close friend. I learned from them that my fever had resulted in my death. I was washed and taken to my upper room. The believers, having heard that Peter was in Lydda, had immediately sent two of our number to get him, for they had heard about the paralysed man who had been healed there[10] and of other healings that Peter had performed in the name of the Lord.[11] Peter, on his arrival here, had found many of the widows mourning. They pointed out to him the clothes that I had made for them and brought many other items to show him. Moved by their tears, their love and their need for me, he had instructed them to leave the room. In the silence, he had prayed and I have returned from death!

How we praised God and how wonderfully God has used this event to bring many more people in Joppa to faith in Christ the Lord. The incident also brought Peter to our town, where he stayed for many days, teaching us and telling us more of Jesus' life, death, resurrection and ascension.

Reflection and discussion

- Did any words or phrases stand out for you?

- Dorcas is likely to have become a believer as a result of Philip's ministry as he travelled north along the coast. Did a certain person play a part in your coming to faith or were several people instrumental in your journey to faith?

- Dorcas had faced adversity: she was a widow. In the monologue, she had the courage to look beyond her grief to the needs of other widows and this became part of the healing process for her. By providing for the disadvantaged, Dorcas was following after God's heart (see Deuteronomy 14:28–29). Dorcas decided to take on the challenge of caring for others rather than waiting for others to care for her. Such a decision took courage. She lived out the words of Jesus, 'Do to others as you would like them to do to you' (Luke 6:31). In doing so, she showed these women, whose loss may have resulted in them feeling abandoned by God, just how much the Lord cared for them. What are the areas of need in our lives? Does this enable us to spot similar needs in others? Pray for the courage to reach out.

- Dorcas' sewing skills had developed as she worked on her innate gifting, gaining knowledge and experience. They took on a new and satisfying dimension as she offered them to the Lord. Read Matthew 25:31–40. Dwell on Jesus' words, 'I'm telling the solemn truth: whenever you did one of these things to someone overlooked or ignored, that was me—you did it to me' (Matthew 25:40, THE MESSAGE). How aware of this truth are we? How can we become more so? Do you feel that you have become more compassionate because of your faith in Christ? How have you responded to this change of heart?

- Faith is the key to being in a right relationship with God (Romans 1:17). However, James made it clear that 'faith by itself, if it is not accompanied by action, is dead' (James 2:17, NIV). What do you understand by these words? Dorcas' life demonstrated that she was a committed follower of the Way. It is of interest that she is referred to as a 'disciple' (Acts 9:36, NIV), the only direct biblical reference to a woman being a disciple.

- Dorcas' talent and skill was her sewing; her instrument of service to God was a needle. What are your skills and talents, your 'instruments of service'? However mundane they may seem, through Dorcas we learn that they can be used for God's purposes to bless others. In what ways could we use our skills and talents, particularly those we consider to be commonplace, to benefit others? Are there creative gifts that you would like to develop further that could bless both you and others? Our Creator God is the source of creativity and of all the joy and blessings that it brings.

- Dorcas wholeheartedly gave of herself and the result was the enrichment of many. In return, she was blessed by their love and commitment to her when a time of crisis came, although this had not been the motivation for her self-giving. Let Jesus' words in Luke 6:38 encourage you. How have you experienced the reality of these words?

- We tend to make artificial divides between the practical and the spiritual, between our working lives and our Christian ministry. How does the life of Dorcas show us that the two are not separate, but go hand in hand? Can you think of examples where we make this needless division? How can this be avoided? Read Romans 12:1. How does this advice enable us to live in a more integrated way?

- We may have great Christian leaders like Philip and Peter, but the heart of the local church is predominantly made up of those who, like Dorcas, love and care for others. Unlike Dorcas, they may not be remembered, but their lives have made a difference. Read Romans 12:6–8. Encourage each other by sharing the gifting that you see in each other.

- A wider good came from this staggering event in Dorcas' life: many believed (Acts 9:42) and the believers in Joppa received teaching from Peter (Acts 9:43). Her life's example has come down through the centuries, inspiring people to acts born of compassion. The Dorcas Society, formed in the nineteenth century and operative in Britain and America, has provided clothing and other practical support to many. How could her example inspire us to help within our communities?

Conclusion

Take time to pray through your findings. What might God be saying to you? Is anything particularly relevant to your life at the moment? Write down what you have learnt and refer back to it regularly in the days ahead so that it becomes part of your thinking, reacting and lifestyle.

Mary of Jerusalem

Introduction

- Read Acts 12:1–19, 25.

- Ask God to speak to you through this episode. You could use the words from 1 Chronicles 29:13–14: 'O Lord, we thank you and praise your glorious name!... Everything we have has come from you. And we give you only what you first gave us!'

- Sit back, relax and close your eyes. Imagine the scene as someone reads the monologue.

Monologue

One by one the believers had arrived at my house under cover of darkness to join us in earnest prayer. We were drawn together by our grief and suffering, for our beloved James had been slain on King Herod Agrippa's orders and Peter was in prison awaiting trial. It was the final day of the feast of unleavened bread, the week of celebrations that followed Passover, a holy week that could not be desecrated by an execution. Jerusalem was full of Jewish visitors—now was an ideal time for Herod Agrippa to win their favour by putting Peter to death. We had heard that the trial would take place the following day. Humanly speaking, there was little prospect of a reprieve.

Our only hope was in our Lord; with one voice we cried out to God for Peter's release. It had been a terrible time of harsh persecution for the believers in Jerusalem, even worse than the first persecution that had followed the stoning of our brother Stephen, a man full of the Holy Spirit, whose faith had inspired us all. At that time, although the apostles had stayed, many other believers had left Jerusalem, for the Pharisee Saul was intent on destroying our Christian community. Both men and women were dragged from their homes and taken to prison.[1] While we prayed for Peter's release, I found myself reflecting on the past: how the escaping Christians had spoken of Jesus wherever they went; how many people had believed their message and been baptised. We had heard reports of the joy with which the good news of Christ was received. Somehow, I mused, God was powerfully at work even in these dreadful times. The words of a psalm came to my mind: 'What joy for those whose strength comes from the Lord, who have set their minds on a pilgrimage to Jerusalem. When they walk through the Valley of Weeping, it will become a place of refreshing springs. The autumn rains will clothe it with blessings. They will continue to grow stronger and each of them will appear before God in Jerusalem. O Lord God of Heaven's Armies, hear my prayer. Listen, O God of Jacob,' I prayed fervently.[2]

Imagine our fear when Saul had returned to Jerusalem, saying that he wished to join the disciples in worship. We were convinced that it was a ploy, a way for him to find out who were the remaining believers and have us slaughtered. It had been my nephew, Barnabas,[3] who had listened to Paul, believed his story, and taken him before the apostles. It was Barnabas who had stood by Saul as the apostles gradually became convinced of the truth of his story.[4]

My dear Joseph Barnabas (for my nephew Joseph was renamed Barnabas by the apostles) was one of the first believers. The name 'Barnabas' means 'son of encouragement'[5] and that suits him perfectly. He always seems to be on the lookout for the person or people who are in need of help. One of his first responses to his faith in Christ was to sell a field and to bring the money to the apostles to be distributed among the poor believers.[6] He was to have a profound influence on my son, John Mark, and I thank God for the relationship between the cousins.

For a while, we believers had a few years of respite in which the church grew greatly and knew peace. Then Herod Agrippa, who had Jewish blood in him but had grown up in Rome, was given power over our area. He wanted to be popular not only with the Romans, but also with the Jews. The surest way to do this was to turn on the followers of Christ and persecute them. His plan was to strike at the heart, to destroy our key leaders—first James, and now Peter.

So there we were, stunned by James' violent death, wondering how we would manage without his leadership and praying wholeheartedly for Peter's release. My home had become a meeting place for the believers, where we comforted each other, worshipped and prayed.

That night we wept at the loss of James and cried out for a miracle for Peter, recalling the events of years before, when the Sadducees had arrested the apostles and had put them in the public jail. An angel had opened the door and brought them out to safety.[7] Those were the days when we still met in the temple and spoke openly in people's homes about Jesus being the Christ. Such days were gone. Our hope was frail: Peter, held in the tower of Antonia, the Roman Garrison on the north-west of the temple, was under the watch of four soldiers at any one time. The circumstances appeared impossible, but still we prayed.

My thoughts and prayers were interrupted by a knock on the gate. I nodded to my servant girl, Rhoda, and she went to see who was there. Fear gripped my heart. Had soldiers come to round up more followers of Jesus? She returned almost immediately, bursting into the room, her face alight with joy. 'Peter is outside!' she said breathlessly.

We thought that the tension of the situation had affected her mind, but she insisted that Peter was at the gate. Then we feared the worst: he had already been killed and his angel had come to tell us. In our confusion, fear and sadness, we could see no other explanation. But then the knocking came again, still quietly but now impatiently. This time I and several others went down with Rhoda and there he was, looking bewildered but solid—Peter! At once we opened the gate to let him in. Exclamations of joy were quickly quelled by Peter as he gestured for us to keep silent. We could not afford to have suspicious neighbours investigating the noise. Locking the gate, we took Peter into the room where he was lovingly embraced. Our tears flowed with our prayers of gratitude.

This is what Peter told us: he was sleeping between two soldiers, his feet and hands chained. How he was sleeping at such a time, I do not know; what a trust in the Lord he must have developed! Suddenly he became aware of a bright light, that he was being shaken and told to get up quickly. Next to him, in the brightness, was an angel of the Lord. As he stood, the chains fell off. The angel instructed him to dress, put on his sandals and wrap his cloak around himself and then to follow. By this stage, Peter believed that he was seeing a vision, so he followed as if in a dream. They passed the first guard, and the second guard—no reaction whatsoever! Then the iron gate into the city opened of its own accord and they started walking down the street. As soon as Peter had worked out where he was, the angel left him.

Peter stood in the dark, feeling the cold night air on his face, assuring himself that this was no dream. An angel of the Lord had been sent to rescue him from Herod! Of course, he knew where most of us would be and so made his way silently through the dark streets. We listened, awestruck. Looking around us, Peter noticed that Jesus' brother, James, was not with us. He instructed us to tell him and the other believers all that had happened. It seems to me now that, in referring to James, he was handing over the leadership of the Jerusalem church into James' hands. He must have realised that it was the right time for him to leave Jerusalem.

The next day we heard of Herod's fury at finding Peter gone. The soldiers could give no explanation and were sentenced to death, according to Roman practice. Herod himself left Jerusalem for Caesarea.

It is not only Barnabas who has influenced my son, John Mark, so strongly; Peter has too. He was always prepared to answer my son's endless questions and shared with John Mark detailed memories of his time with Jesus. My son was later to write these down.[8] In many ways, Peter became a father figure to John Mark, certainly spiritually.[9] (John, meaning 'God is gracious', is my son's Hebrew name, and like many, he also had a Latin name, Mark.) His life has been shaped by these men who taught and prayed in our home. It should not have surprised me therefore when John Mark told me of his invitation to travel with Barnabas and Paul, spreading the gospel. Barnabas and Paul had recently brought gifts from the believers in Antioch, for Judea had been hit by famine and many in the city of Jerusalem were in great need. Trusting Barnabas wholeheartedly, I agreed, and my son, barely out of childhood, went with them to Antioch.[10]

It was some time before I saw him again. He had been assisting Paul and Barnabas in the work that the Holy Spirit had set them apart for, carrying the good news of Christ to Cyprus. Then, to my surprise, John Mark returned to Jerusalem alone, leaving Barnabas and Paul to continue their travels. What exactly had happened, I do not know to this day; it seems that there was some disagreement.[11]

Two years passed before Paul and Barnabas returned, as did Peter, for an important council meeting that was to take place in Jerusalem.[12] Challenged by their visit, John Mark was keen to join Paul and Barnabas once again. By then, Paul and Barnabas had gone on to Antioch and were planning to revisit the churches in order to strengthen and encourage them. But Paul refused to take my son with him in view of what had happened before. I could sense my son's hurt and disappointment. However, Barnabas, perhaps through principle, perhaps through family loyalty, came and took John Mark back to Cyprus with him.[13] I see now that all worked for good, for while they continued their ministry in Cyprus, Paul chose Silas to accompany him, and the good news of Christ travelled even further afield. I took delight in the knowledge that my son was playing an important part in the growth of the church and was such a help to many, including Peter. My joy was deep when I learned of John Mark's reconciliation with Paul[14] and of the way in which Paul eventually came to value his support and company.

Reflection and discussion

- Did any words or phrases stand out for you?

- Mary is another biblical woman who regularly opened up her home to others—Peter knew exactly where to find the believers. She offered her home as a place of prayer, worship and mutual support. Mary showed great courage in doing this, for there were huge risks involved. It was a time of persecution and she must have known the possible cost. She was also conceivably endangering her son, which would have been a great concern for her. Mary had made a courageous decision: 'to seek the kingdom of God above all else, and live righteously' (Matthew 6:33). Read some ways we can live righteously in Romans 12:9–15. What do you think it means to 'take delight in honouring one another'? (v. 10)

- Some of the early disciples felt called to give their home, possessions and land. Read Acts 4:32–36. Others, like Mary, made their wealth available to others through keeping but sharing their homes. We prayed at the start of this study, 'Everything we have has come from you, and we give you only what you first gave us' (1 Chronicles 29:14). In today's society, how do we live this out in practice? We need wisdom to know how to use all that we have received for God's glory.

- Barnabas, Mary and John Mark (who later in his life encouraged both Peter and Paul) were a family of encouragers. To encourage means to put courage within somebody—to hearten and cheer, to inspire and reassure, to boost and embolden. Based on these definitions, share times when you have been encouraged and consider ways you can encourage others.

- In the monologue Mary, ponders on how God had used the previous persecution for his purposes, for through the scattering of Jesus' followers, the good news had spread. Read Paul's testimony in Philippians 1:12–14. Pray for those who are persecuted today, that they will have the strength to stand firm in their faith and that God's kingdom will continue to grow.

- The believers praying for Peter's release demonstrated both faith and a lack of faith! They had enough faith to pray and remember past answers to prayer, but not enough faith to believe that the man at the door was Peter, mistakenly thinking that he was an angel. The characters in the Bible are not 'superheroes', but very real and, like us, are full of contradictions. They had seen faith-inspiring miracles, but had also witnessed the deaths of Stephen and James. We, too, have our highs and lows that can threaten our faith. If you are able, share these. We often need to pray like the man who asked Jesus for healing for his son: 'I do believe, but help me overcome my unbelief!' (Mark 9:24). Meditate on the wonderful promise in Isaiah 65:24.

- In the monologue, it is imagined that Mary prayed using the words of Psalm 84. It can be very helpful when we do not know how to pray to use the prayers of others, such as the psalms. These cover the whole spectrum of human emotions and give hope, even in tough situations, by reminding us of God's presence with us and his past actions on behalf of his people. Share prayers and psalms that have helped you.

- The believers had gathered together in Mary's home to pray for Peter's release. We read in James 5:16 that 'the earnest prayer of a righteous person has great power and produces wonderful results'. Jesus promised, 'Where two or three come together in my name, there am I with them,' (Matthew 18:19, NIV). More than this, Jesus is actually interceding with God on our behalf (Hebrews 7:25). Do you have opportunity to pray with others? If not, is there a way that you could build this habit into your life? Share times when praying with others has been helpful, particularly times when you have seen amazing answers to earnest prayer.

- Mary had a crucial role in bringing up John Mark. He had seen her practical and risk-taking Christian living and was keen to accompany Paul and Barnabas on their challenging journeys to spread the good news of Jesus. We do not know from the Bible narrative what went wrong between John Mark and Paul, but it was logical for him to return home to where he had Mary's support. Mary provided him with a bolt-hole where he could come to terms with and recover from what had taken place. Share people who have done this for you or times when you have been able to do this for others.

- John Mark may have run away from a difficult situation before, for some scholars believe that he is the young man in Mark's Gospel who ran away at Jesus' arrest (Mark 14:51–52). Personal maturity takes time to develop; lessons can be learnt and wisdom gained from the mistakes that we make. Barnabas had the patience to stand by John Mark and give him another chance, believing in his potential. To whom can we be a Barnabas in this way?

Conclusion

Take time to pray through your findings. What might God be saying to you? Is anything particularly relevant to your life at the moment? Write down what you have learnt and refer back to it regularly in the days ahead so that it becomes part of your thinking, reacting and lifestyle.

Lydia

Introduction

- Read Acts 16:11–40.

- Ask God to speak to you through this episode. You could use the words from Philippians 1:6: 'And I am certain that God, who began the good work within you, will continue his work until it is finally finished on the day when Christ Jesus returns.'

- Sit back, relax and close your eyes. Imagine the scene as someone reads the monologue.

Monologue

When I arrived at Philippi, I became known as the Lydian woman, and gradually as Lydia. You see, I had been born and raised in the city of Thyatira, in the province of Lydia in Asia. Thyatira was famous for its purple dye, an extremely expensive dye made from the excretions of the Murex snail. The Romans loved to wear tunics and cloaks made of purple; it gave them a mark of superiority, of nobility. I had become a dealer in purple cloth at a young age and, realising its potential, developed my business further, making a large profit. As a wealthy woman, I was in the minority. I had no need to marry and could make my own choices concerning my future. I made two decisions that fundamentally changed the direction of my life. The first was to convert to Judaism. There were many Jewish people in Thyatira; I respected their way of life, their morality, their business sense. But more than that, I respected their faith: a belief in the one God, creator and sustainer. I found this faith more convincing than belief in the many gods worshipped throughout the city. It made more sense: the Jewish history was to me far more believable, more human, than the stories of the Roman gods. So I attended their synagogue, adopted their faith and learned to fear God, living in obedience to the Jewish laws.

My second decision was to move to Philippi in the region of Macedonia. This was a business choice. Philippi, on the important Via Egnatia, the trade route linking the world of Rome to the east, is like a bridge between them that has to be crossed. As a centre of commerce, it is a place where my cloth is in great demand and can be traded in many directions. Philippi has been a Roman colony since it was last fought over around 100 years ago. The city is beautiful, boasting the best of Roman architecture and building skills: the grand road in and out; the Theatre, Forum and Acropolis; sports facilities, temples and courts. At each end there is a gate: the Krenides gate leading to the river of that name and the Neapolis gate, leading to the port of Neapolis. Surrounded by fertile land, agriculture as well as trade flourishes.

My business thrived. I had all the trappings of success: a large house and household of servants; clothes and food; the respect and admiration of those who mattered in Philippian society. However, Philippi had such a small Jewish community, not even the ten men required by the authorities for the building of a synagogue. So we had to meet beyond the Krenides gate, down by the river. There I would join a few other women to pray on the sabbath. My life was so full and yet I felt so thirsty for more; the words 'As the deer longs for streams of water, so I long for you, O God',[1] often filled my thoughts as we prayed. Those times of prayer down by the river were the foundation of my life, giving me a much-needed break from the demands of business and a means of maintaining perspective.

I was at this time of prayer when four men arrived and, surprisingly, joined us in prayer: a Jewish man named Paul, who came from the city of Tarsus, and his three travelling companions—Silas, a young man named Timothy and a doctor called Luke. Being the sabbath, they had enquired as to whether any Jews lived in the city and, if so, where they met to worship, and had been directed to the river. They sat down and told us why they were there—how, while in Troas, Paul had been directed by God through a vision in which a man had beckoned him to go to Macedonia to help the people.[2] So they travelled by boat via Samothrace to Neapolis, and then made their way to Philippi. As Paul continued, he spoke to my heart's longings; perhaps my prayers were being answered through these men. Deep within me, their words satisfied as water quenches thirst. First, Paul spoke of Jewish history. Next, he explained that the long-awaited Messiah had come. He told us that this Messiah, this Saviour, was Jesus; but rather than welcoming him, the Jewish leaders had rejected him, turned him over to the Romans, who had crucified him. My tears flowed: the Messiah had come and gone, all was lost.

Paul spoke of his burial and then, to my amazement, of God raising Jesus from the dead. Many had seen him, many who were still alive and could testify to the resurrection. These men saw it as their God-given task to spread the good news throughout the world, baptising people in the name of God the Father, his son Jesus and the Holy Spirit. With every word he spoke, a 'yes' resounded in my soul. It was as if all my life had been leading to that point. The men explained that those who believed in Jesus received forgiveness, life eternal and the Holy Spirit, who had been promised by Jesus as a helper, a comforter, a counsellor who would empower his followers and be with them, even in them.[3] I believed and asked if I too could be baptised along with my household. I persuaded the men to make my home theirs while they were in Philippi. We had so much to learn, and they agreed to stay.

Initially the visit went smoothly enough, but then Paul started receiving opposition from a slave girl who had a spirit of divination. Seeing into the future was important to the Romans, although forbidden by God in the scriptures. This girl earned her owners a great deal of money. Paul became increasingly uneasy because each day she would follow him, shouting out that they were servants of the Most High and had come to tell the people of Philippi how they could be saved. He was worried that God's work would be linked in some way to her and that this would ruin the reputation of the small but growing number of believers, causing us trouble. In his concern, he called out in the name of Jesus that the spirit of divination would leave her. Immediately the spirit departed and she was calm. Her owners were furious because their means of earning money had gone, so they took Paul and Silas to the marketplace to stand before the two magistrates. They reported that Paul and Silas were causing a disturbance and were encouraging the people of Philippi to follow customs that were unlawful to the Romans. The gathering crowd joined in the verbal attack on them. Instructed by the magistrates, their assistants stripped Paul and Silas and used their wooden rods to beat them unrestrainedly, while the people roared their approval. It was awful to watch, an agony not to be able to intervene. I knew that the magistrates' response was far too harsh. Paul and Silas were then taken to the inner prison reserved for the most dangerous prisoners and placed in stocks.

Of course, it was widely known that these four men were my guests. But in spite of my high profile within the city, I could not help them. I could only hope and pray for their release.

That night, at about midnight, there was a substantial earthquake in the prison area which was sufficient to cause damage to the foundations. It was quite localised; we were aware of the tremor in the residential area, although the buildings were unscathed. God was at work that night, but it was not until late the next morning when, to our astonishment, Paul and Silas arrived at my house, that we found out what had taken place in the jail. Their story was amazing. They had been praying and worshipping God, the other prisoners and jailer listening closely, when the quake struck. Their chains had broken and the door had swung open! Paul had gathered the prisoners around him. Waking from sleep, the jailer, knowing the torturous death he would go through when it was discovered that the prisoners had escaped, had drawn his sword to kill himself. Paul had prevented him, reassuring him that all of the prisoners were there. A light had been called for and then the jailer had seen the evidence for himself. He had fallen down at Paul's and Silas' feet, asking them about the salvation of which they had been singing and praying. In faith, he had responded to their words, taking Paul and Silas into his home, tending to their wounds. He had asked to be baptised with his household. Then, in the middle of the night, they had celebrated over a meal. All this had been going on while I had been praying and sleeping fitfully!

The next day Paul and Silas had been told by the magistrates that they could leave, as their punishment was over. However, Paul had terrified them by telling them that they were Roman citizens. They should never have been beaten or imprisoned without a fair trial. He had said that he would drop the matter only if they received a formal apology and if their names were completely cleared of any shame. He wished the magistrates to come to the prison in person and accompany them out. This the magistrates had done, asking them to leave the city.

So they had come to my house. Paul encouraged us and, confident that there was no stain on the reputation of the believers, did as the magistrates had requested and left. As for me, I was in an ideal situation to spread the good news; the cloth traders listened to me, taking their stories with them on their journeys. I had endless opportunities to speak to clients buying their purple linen, the colour of royalty, the colour of the robe that the Roman soldiers had placed on Jesus of Nazareth,[4] King of the Jews, my King of Kings and Lord of Lords.

Reflection and discussion

- Did any words or phrases stand out for you?

- Read Acts 16:6–10. The Holy Spirit blocked Paul and his companions from taking certain courses of action and opened up another. When we pray for guidance, we can ask God to 'block' or 'bless'. Guidance includes both going in a certain direction and being kept away from others. What is your experience of this? The great significance of this account is that it was the first move of Christianity into Europe. According to the biblical account, Lydia was the first European Christian. Share times when God has brought blessings from an unexpected change in direction.

- In the monologue, Lydia found that her successful business, although rewarding, was not sufficiently fulfilling; neither was her worship of God, although this was of fundamental importance to her. There was still a spiritual need to be met and this was satisfied as she heard about and responded to Jesus Christ. Lydia was a genuine seeker after God, as Cornelius had been.[5] God always honours the searching heart. Jesus' brother James wrote, 'Come near to God and he will come near to you' (James 4:8, NIV). Lydia's heart was softened; she was ready to learn and receive. Read Jesus' promise in Luke 11:9–13. Lydia's search originally brought her to Judaism and then to the gospel of Christ. What can we learn from this? Ask God to make us aware of those around us who are spiritually searching and who have hearts softened towards him.

- Lydia prioritised sabbath worship in spite of her business demands. It is easy to go off track when we are surrounded by pressures, and for our faith and its practise to gradually become less central. Luke, whom Lydia befriended, wrote an account of Jesus' parable of the sower. Read this in Luke 8:4–15. If we are honest, what pressures and pleasures tend to draw us away, preventing us from maturing and becoming fruitful?

- The good seed falling on good ground produces crops and fruit. As soon as Lydia received Christ, she shared him with her household. We do not know if her whole household became Christians immediately. The baptisms were, however, a sign of her home now being a Christian household and a Christian community. Further fruit was evident in Lydia as she cared for her new friends by offering hospitality. She demonstrated a 'noble and good heart' who '[heard] the word, [retained] it and by persevering [produced] a good crop' (Luke 8:15, NIV). Read Galatians 5:22–23. Consider the fruit you are bearing and/or would like to bear.

- Lydia had already shown courage both in her life as a business-woman and in identifying herself with a minority religion, rejecting the prevailing culture around her. She then encouraged these foreigners to stay with her. There seems to have been no self-interest, no anxiety for her business or fear as to what would happen to her reputation as a result of her identification with this new group of people, called Christians. Indeed, she was at the core of this group; probably the Philippian believers met in her home. Lydia seemed to be wholehearted in all that she did. We are so often blown this way and that. What can we learn from her courage?

- Lydia demonstrated further courage when she welcomed Paul and Silas back into her home after their imprisonment, ignoring any social stigma. By this stage, she had seen that following Christ would bring spiritual opposition and possibly physical danger. What forms does opposition take in your life experience? Read Luke 9:23–25 and Romans 1:16. Do we have this courage? If not, how can we grow in our convictions and their application?

- By AD62, one decade later, a whole church had sprung up in Philippi. Paul wrote to this church remembering the women who had helped him, which must have included Lydia (Philippians 4:3). He remembers with gratitude their gifts to him.[6] It is likely that, as a wealthy woman, Lydia would have contributed to this. The letter to the Philippians also includes an early doxology, possibly used by Lydia along with the other Christians, one which we are still drawing on in song, prayer and declaration of faith today. Read this and the advice to the growing church in Philippi in Philippians 2:1–11. What stands out to you in these verses?

- Paul writes that he was shamefully treated in Philippi (1 Thessalonians 2:2). Presumably if Lydia had known that Paul was a Roman citizen, she could have spoken up for him. It is likely that his father had become a Roman citizen by payment or service, and therefore Paul, although a Jew, was also a Roman citizen by birth. Paul saw the necessity of protecting his own reputation and hence that of Lydia and the newly formed group of Christians. Not wanting them to be viewed as those who mixed with lawbreakers or troublemakers, he spoke out and demanded vindication. There are times to be silent and times when we have to stand up and speak out to protect our reputation or that of others. Have there been times when you have done this? What was the outcome? How do we discern when to speak and when to remain silent?

Conclusion

Take time to pray through your findings. What might God be saying to you? Is anything particularly relevant to your life at the moment? Write down what you have learnt and refer back to it regularly in the days ahead so that it becomes part of your thinking, reacting and lifestyle.

Priscilla

Introduction

- Read Acts 18:1–28; Romans 16:3–5; 1 Corinthians 16:19; and 2 Timothy 4:19.

- Ask God to speak to you through this episode. You could use the words from Ephesians 3:20: 'Now all glory to God, who is able, through the mighty power at work within us, to accomplish infinitely more than we might ask or think.'

- Sit back, relax and close your eyes. Imagine the scene as someone reads the monologue.

Monologue

I wonder sometimes what it would be like to live one's life in the same place and to be rooted among one group of people for a lifetime. This has been far from my experience.

My husband Aquila and I lived in Rome as part of the Jewish community. We were tent-makers there; Aquila made the goat-skinned tent coverings and I tended to make smaller leather goods. Tents were in demand to house the soldiers and for other military uses, so there was plenty of work. The Jewish community in Rome was being stirred up by extraordinary talk arriving with traders—the Messiah had come as a man named Jesus; he had been put to death in Jerusalem and yet came back to life three days later. I was intrigued by their ideas and could follow their logic as they explained how the scriptures pointed to Jesus as being the long-awaited

Messiah. My husband and I were both gaining in our understanding when trouble broke out. It is not surprising that there would be dissension between the Jews who did not believe in Jesus and those who did. The arguments escalated, turning into riots. Claudius took radical action, ordering all Jews to leave the city of Rome. It was a harrowing time for us.

We, like many Jews, chose Corinth as our destination. Corinth, built on an isthmus between two seaports, had a status comparable to Rome itself. The ancient city had been rebuilt and developed as a Roman colony about 100 years ago. We reasoned that we would feel at home there and do good business.

Our tent-making trade prospered and we quickly became well settled. Then one day a man named Paul arrived at our home. He had travelled from Athens and wished to work alongside us, as he was also a tent-maker. We invited him to stay with us and, as we worked, we discussed every subject under the sun. Our main topic of conversation concerned Jesus of Nazareth. Paul told us his life story: how he had persecuted Christians, then of his meeting with Jesus on the road to Damascus and its life-changing impact, and of the increasing number of people following the Way.[1] Our hearts were touched and we, too, became Christians. Paul imparted his knowledge and understanding, and we became truly grounded in Christian beliefs, experiencing the work of the Holy Spirit in our lives and community. Each sabbath, we would go to the synagogue where Paul would reason with both Jews and Greeks regarding the fulfilment of the scriptures in Jesus. I treasure those days.

In time, Paul's friends and companions, Silas and Timothy, came to join us. They had been visiting the church community in Macedonia and brought with them financial gifts for Paul from the Christians there.[2] This enabled Paul to focus on his ministry, so he left our home and went to stay with a Gentile worshipper of God named Titius Justus, who was keen to spend time with Paul and learn more about Jesus. Ironically, his house was next door to the synagogue, for Paul had been on the receiving end of increasing opposition from the Jews. The more he testified that Jesus was the Christ, the angrier they became. Finally, Paul decided that he had fulfilled his responsibility to tell them about Jesus, so he placed them into God's hands—they were responsible for their response to Christ and would be judged by it. His plan was to focus on preaching to the Greek Gentiles. But, just as he had despaired of reaching the Jewish community in Corinth, there was a breakthrough. The synagogue leader, Crispus, along with his household, believed in the Lord Jesus and were baptised. Perhaps his example freed many others to take their steps of faith, for many believed and were baptised.

We became aware how worn out Paul had become; he was ready to leave Corinth. But, at his lowest ebb, the Lord spoke to him in a vision, telling him to stay and promising him safety, for there were many in the city who would become the Lord's. With this encouragement, Paul lived among us for a year, teaching and training us.

Opposition was never far around corner, however, and many Jews remained hostile to him. Eventually they brought charges to the governor, Gallio, stating that Paul was encouraging people to worship in a way contrary to Jewish law. Before Paul could defend himself, Gallio declared with irritation that this was a religious dispute and had nothing to do with him. He had the Jews thrown out of court. Once more Paul was vindicated, although he still had many enemies. On one occasion we were in a position to save his life. As God had promised, he kept Paul safe. Eventually, Paul believed that it was time to leave Corinth. As he prepared and talked to us about the next stage of his journey, it became clear to us that we should accompany him to Ephesus.

So once more we moved and settled in a new city. We were to end up staying in Ephesus while Paul continued on his journey. Using all that we had learnt, we both taught and built up the believers in their faith. We attended the synagogue, speaking of Jesus whenever and wherever we had opportunity.

It was then that God brought Apollos into our lives. He was a highly intelligent and educated man from the university city of Alexandria in Egypt, the city second only to Rome. Apollos' knowledge of the scriptures was extensive. His passion for the Lord and his teaching about Jesus was accurate; he spoke out boldly in the synagogue. But Aquila and I sensed that something was missing; as we listened to him, we came to understand that he knew only the baptism of John.[3] This was the baptism of repentance for purification from sin and not the baptism commanded by Jesus—baptism in the name of the Father, the Son and the Holy Spirit.[4]

We were concerned for Apollos, wanting him to know deeper spiritual truths. Jesus' cousin, John, had taught that the Lord was so much greater than him that he was not worthy even to untie the straps on his sandals. Jesus would come, he explained, baptising with the Holy Spirit and with fire.[5] Christian baptism, we told Apollos, was so much more than repentance. We were baptised into the death of Jesus, buried with him as we went below the water, and then raised with Christ as we emerged from the water. Baptism was a symbol of what had taken place within us. We then walked in 'newness of life';[6] in fact, we now lived *in* Christ by the power of the Holy Spirit. It was not just a matter of knowing about Jesus and his teaching. Paul had taught us that through baptism we put on Christ.[7] There was a freedom in the Spirit that we longed for Apollos to experience for himself.[8] Christ had set us free and we no longer needed to live as slaves to the law.[9]

It was such a joy to watch a transformation take place in Apollos as we spent time with him. We saw how much he could offer the community in Corinth, and as Apollos seemed to have a God-given longing to go there, we readily wrote letters to the church we loved so much, recommending him to them. We knew that, with his wonderful debating and oratory skills, he would be able to refute the Jews' arguments in public, proving through the scriptures that the Messiah had come in the person of Jesus. Apollos became such a blessing to the Christians in Corinth, building them up and becoming one of their leaders. He possessed such gifts that the church there was in danger of following Apollos rather than God. Paul had to write to them asserting that it is God that we follow, not man. God causes growth; we only plant seeds and nurture them.[10]

This is what Aquila and I understood our ministry to be: planting and nurturing seeds. Although settled and busy shepherding the Christians at Ephesus, Aquila and I missed Rome. So when we heard that the attitude towards the Jews in Rome had relaxed after the death of Claudius, we decided to return there. We quickly became involved in supporting the Christian community that started to meet in our home, but we were not to stay. Nero commenced a ruthless and cruel persecution of the Christians. We remained for as long as we were able, but eventually felt called by God to return to Ephesus. There we joined Timothy in his ministry and in fervent prayer for Paul, who by this time was imprisoned in Rome. We knew from his letter to Timothy that we were never far from his thoughts.[11]

Footnote

Tradition tells us that Priscilla and Aquila eventually died as martyrs.

Reflection and discussion

- Did any words or phrases stand out for you?

- Uprooting, moving home and settling elsewhere takes courage, particularly if we have known happiness and meaningful relationships in the place that is being left, and even more so if the move is enforced by influences beyond our control. Priscilla and Aquila moved for various reasons: the decrees of Rome; to support Paul; in response to a leading from God; and to escape persecution. The continual upheaval for Aquila and Priscilla required both the courage to face change and loss, and the resilience to endure it and adapt. Reflect together on moves you have made during your lives, perhaps some were joyful and easy to adapt to, perhaps others were in difficult circumstances. How has your faith made a difference? Read Deuteronomy 31:8 and Psalm 139:1–10.

- Once they had come to faith, Aquila and Priscilla committed their lives to supporting the group of Christian believers wherever they went, opening their home to them. They combined this with their working life. It can be difficult on occasions to balance the different aspects of our lives. Share your experiences of this, particularly ways in which you have achieved a more helpful and sustainable balance.

- Having been equipped by Paul, Aquila and Priscilla were able to 'plant and nurture' seed together. This couple had a joint calling to leadership, in their case as a married couple. Joint (or team) leadership has the benefit of mutual support. Leaders can complement each other's gifting and provide more stability for those in their care. Read Ecclesiastes 4:9–12. They can also sharpen each other's thinking. Read Proverbs 27:17. What do you understand from these verses? Priscilla and Aquila had a joint purpose, a shared faith, deep fellowship and the ability to work together, giving all that they had to expand God's kingdom. Pray for these attributes for yourself and for those you live and work closely with in formal and informal roles.

- Priscilla's name is usually mentioned first; the most likely reason for this unusual occurrence is that she was of a higher social status. It is likely therefore that she was an educated woman and was well able to work alongside her husband in nurturing and teaching the Christians. In Galatians 3:28 we read, 'In Christ's family there can be no division into Jew and non-Jew, slave and free, male and female. Among us you are all equal. That is, we are all in a common relationship with Jesus Christ' (*THE MESSAGE*). The old divisions of superiority and inferiority are abolished in Christ. It took courage for Priscilla to go against the expected role for women and to work alongside her husband in an equal partnership. Feelings of inferiority and social pressure can hinder us from flourishing as

God intended. Share your experiences of this and of how God has worked in your life through the Holy Spirit. During the week take time to meditate on 2 Corinthians 5:17.

- We see Priscilla's sensitivity and insight in the way that they took Apollos into their home to speak to him privately, developing his faith and understanding. How has learning in an informal setting such as a home changed your understanding and enabled you to grow in your faith?

- Priscilla and Aquila saw the potential in Apollos: he was a scholar, an orator and a debater. They helped him on his spiritual journey, empowering him through their nurturing, so that he could use his gifts more fully to defend Christianity. Which Christians do you know who God has placed in high positions where they can reason on an intellectual level for Christ? Pray for them, particularly for wisdom in challenging the spiritual, moral and ethical matters that they discuss.

- Priscilla was aware that her influence on others for the growth of God's kingdom was by God's grace. It is vital to give God the glory and not to take it for ourselves. The church in Corinth was in danger of following Apollos or Paul rather than God. Read 1 Corinthians 3:3–9. Further on in the letter Paul states, 'By the grace of God I am what I am, and his grace to me was not without effect' (1 Corinthians 15:10, NIV). Pray that you will be able to influence others in a positive way, as Priscilla did, maintaining a humility that recognises God's grace in all things.

Conclusion

Take time to pray through your findings. What might God be saying to you? Is anything particularly relevant to your life at the moment? Write down what you have learnt and refer back to it regularly in the days ahead so that it becomes part of your thinking, reacting and lifestyle.

Phoebe

Introduction

- Read Romans 16:1–2; Romans 12:1—13:2.

- Ask God to speak to you through this episode. You could use the words from Romans 15:13: 'I pray that God, the source of hope, will fill you completely with joy and peace because you trust in him. Then you will overflow with confident hope through the power of the Holy Spirit.'

- Sit back, relax and close your eyes. Imagine the scene as someone reads the monologue.

Monologue

My name is Phoebe and I used to live in Cenchrea, the town to the east of Corinth and a port for that city. Cenchrea is a town that bustles both with people and ideas, bursting with travellers' tales as well as with the vice and immorality often found in ports. However, I now live in Rome, at least for the time being. Maybe one day I shall return to Cenchrea. I have only recently arrived and settled in Rome, the city at the centre of the world. This is my account of how I came to be here.

About eight years ago I became a follower of the Way. A man named Paul had come to Corinth[1] and lived there for one and a half years.[2] He had brought with him the good news of Jesus Christ and a group of believers had sprung up as a result of his teaching. Two other men, Silas and Timothy, joined him, and together they explained to the

Jews and Gentiles how they could become Christians, one in Christ. Their teaching was revolutionary to both groups. The Jews, waiting for the Messiah, were being told that the Messiah had already come in the person of Jesus. The Gentiles were being taught that there was *one* God and that he had become a man, and lived on earth. Gradually the message of the good news spread east of Corinth and so it was that a group of believers sprang up in Cenchrea. There Paul, Silas and Timothy witnessed to us, teaching us and building up our faith.

When Paul knew that it was time for him to leave Corinth, he stayed awhile in Cenchrea awaiting a ship to take him to Ephesus. He had been seeking the Lord's blessing on the next stage of his journey. As a symbol of this inner listening and submission to God's ways, Paul had taken a thirty day Nazarite vow which was completed while he was with us.[3] So he shaved his head and sacrificed his hair.[4] The Jewish Christians were impressed that he chose to adhere to this scriptural vow.

In that time, I had got to know Paul well. He was a brother to me and I a trusted sister to him. He was not to return to Corinth and Cenchrea for six years. In the meantime, I immersed myself in the teaching and life of the church. I had both the means to help financially and the strength and knowledge to minister as a diakonos to those in the church.

I welcomed Paul's return.[5] His plan was to stay for three months over the winter, while sea travel was dangerous, and then to sail to Syria and on to Jerusalem.[6] He explained that eventually his aim was to go to Rome. In preparation for this visit, he wrote a letter to the church in Rome in which he expressed the truths of the gospel, wanting both Jews and Gentiles to have a firm grounding in their faith, one that would unite them and pave the way for his ministry there. As he told me of the letter, I realised its importance, for it spoke of the heart of the Gospel: we all have sinned;[7] we are lost without God;[8] Christ died for all;[9] all who accept Christ are pardoned[10] if they acknowledge

Christ;[11] they become children of God and can experience the presence, power and gifting of the Holy Spirit.[12] I knew that his letter would be crucial in teaching the Christians in Rome how to live and how to respond to the Roman authorities.

Life does not always work out as we would hope, however, for Paul's hopes of going to Rome were not to be fulfilled for several years and would happen in a most unexpected way.[13]

The three months with us were cut short, for we heard rumours of a plot that had been made against Paul by some Jews. It was wise for him to depart quickly, so he decided to return by land through Macedonia rather than sail for Syria.[14] But before doing so, he entrusted me with what I now consider to have been the most important commission of my life: to carry the letter by hand, to be his representative to the church in Rome. I felt both honoured and daunted by the task.

Paul was deeply concerned that the church in Rome should welcome and accept me. He wanted them to help me to settle in a new city and Christian community where I longed to be of service. In his letter he asked them to treat me with respect and love.

So we parted ways. Once the weather had improved, my journey took me oversea to Italy and then up the great Appian Way, the road from the south of Italy straight to Rome itself. I treasured those scrolls as I travelled. How I prayed for that letter—that it would get to them safely, that it would bring wisdom to the church and be a blessing to them.

I will never forget my first view of Rome and the hills surrounding it. The city itself took my breath away: the beauty of the Tiber flowing through the city; the Forum; the theatres and fine buildings. As I entered the city, I prayed that I would be able to place the scrolls into the hands of the Christians, that it would be accepted and bear much fruit. God has answered my prayers.

Footnote

Although we cannot be absolutely sure that Phoebe took Paul's letter to Rome, it is widely believed that she did; there must have been a very good reason for her to leave Cenchrea and travel to Rome. Paul's commendation in Romans 16:1-2 is further evidence.

Reflection and discussion

- Did any words or phrases stand out for you?

- The Greek name Phoebe means 'radiant or shining one'. Phoebe may have been a Greek or Jewish Christian, as many Jewish Christians also took on Greek names. She lived up to her name in that her lifestyle brightly reflected the Lord. Paul said of her, 'She has been a great help to many people, including me' (Romans 16:2, NIV). Read 2 Corinthians 3:18 and 4:5-7. This outward 'shining' is a result of an inward and ongoing 'heart' transformation. Our radiance may only be skin-deep at times; we wear an outward smile that belies the struggle within. What might be the causes of this? How can we develop radiance from within?

- The word 'help', referring to Phoebe in Romans 16:2, can also be translated as 'benefactor', 'succour' and 'patron'. It seems likely, therefore, that Phoebe gave hospitality and made her wealth available to those in need, as well as helping in many other ways. It was a great honour at that time to be called a benefactor because the emperor was known as the state supreme benefactor. Today, we are often measured by what we have achieved rather than by what we have contributed to the lives of others. Positions involving caring may be overlooked and undervalued. Wealth is often used for self-gratification rather than for acts of compassion. Read Jesus' parable in Luke 12:15-21. How do Phoebe's lifestyle choices challenge us? What changes can we make? How can we affirm those in caring roles?

- Phoebe was a 'diakonos' (Romans 16:1). There is much debate as to whether the word 'diakonos' referred to a formal or an informal position within the church, for 'diakonos' is used as both a general term for a servant or minister, but is also used for a formal position in church leadership. Whether she was a female deacon or not, she gave of herself generously, playing an important role within the church. Read the qualities to look for, found in 1 Timothy 3:1–13, when choosing church leaders. These would have been qualities that Phoebe possessed and are ones for us to aspire to in our Christian walk. Pray for these qualities to be present in the lives of our church leaders.

- Paul completed his Nazarite vow—a sign of his sincerity, thanksgiving and desire to know God's will and favour—while he was in Cenchrea (Acts 18:18). By taking this vow, he had shown the Jews that one could choose to follow Old Testament customs voluntarily as long as the same customs were not enforced on others, particularly on Gentile believers. Can you think of Old Testament and New Testament traditions that fall into this category today? These could be of importance to some Christians in their walk with God but are not necessarily ones that should be enforced on other people. Read 1 Corinthians 9:19–23. Paul was prepared to be all things to all people in order to advance the gospel and to 'obey the law of Christ' (v. 21). What is the law of Christ and how do we obey it in practice?

- It is generally accepted that Paul entrusted Phoebe with the huge responsibility of taking his letter to the Romans. He must have believed this lady to be strong and capable. No doubt he had been impressed with her stability and loyal service to the Christians in Cenchrea during the six years of his absence. Our current life experiences often prepare us for what lies ahead, developing our character so that we are ready for the next challenge. Share times when you have found this to be true.

- It must have taken great courage for Phoebe to undertake the lengthy and potentially dangerous journey to Rome, particularly as she was a single woman without the protection of a husband. Moreover, she did not know how she would be received by the Christians on her arrival, and was dependent on their response to Paul's commendation. Share times when you have needed courage to fulfil a responsibility or make a difficult journey. Have there been occasions when you have had to face people and been unsure of the reception that you would receive? How did you prepare and pray?

- We do not know whether Phoebe was still in Rome by the time Paul was taken there under armed guard (AD60). In the monologue, we see that the letter to the Romans prepared the way for Paul's ministry in Rome, covering many important aspects of Christian understanding. Rome was crucial in God's plan: it was the city from which the gospel could spread rapidly, a city of huge influence throughout the world. Paul's intention to go to Spain and Rome seemed to be part of his strategic plan, no doubt led by the Holy Spirit (Romans 15:23–24). How do we balance planning for the future with being led by God through the Holy Spirit? Share from your experiences. What insights do you gain from Proverbs 30:24–25, Galatians 5:16, 25 and James 4:13–16?

Conclusion

Take time to pray through your findings. What might God be saying to you? Is anything particularly relevant to your life at the moment? Write down what you have learnt and refer back to it regularly in the days ahead so that it becomes part of your thinking, reacting and lifestyle.

Eunice

Introduction

- Read Acts 14:5–23; 16:1–5; 2 Timothy 1:1–8; 3:14–17.

- Ask God to speak to you through these scriptures. You could use the words from Hebrews 13:21: 'May he equip you with all you need for doing his will. May he produce in you, through the power of Jesus Christ, every good thing that is pleasing to him.'

- Sit back, relax and close your eyes. Imagine the scene as someone reads the monologue.

We do not know exactly when Eunice and Timothy became Christians, but it is likely that it was on Paul's first missionary journey and visit to Lystra.

Monologue

How I rejoice that God, through his Spirit's guiding, sent Paul here to Lystra where we live. Lystra is but a small town high up on the plains, an outpost of Roman defence 25 miles south of the city of Iconium. It is perhaps the safety of its insignificance that attracted Paul and his companion Barnabas to us, for they had left Iconium in a hurry after they had been attacked by the leaders and an antagonistic crowd.

Their arrival was to change not only my life, but the lives of many in this town. There were a considerable number of Jews and Greeks living peaceably together in Lystra. Indeed, I had married a Greek.

I had been born into a Jewish family and my mother, Lois, was devout in following our faith. My earliest memories are of her telling me the stories of the Israelites, teaching me God's commandments and explaining to me his plan for his people—how they were awaiting the coming of his Anointed One. This went deep into my heart, mind and soul.

When my husband and I were blessed with a son, Timothy, it was my desire and aim to provide the same rich teaching for him. Timothy would listen for hours to me and his grandmother, his perceptive nature attuning him to the plight of his people and their hope for the future. My husband was happy for us to influence Timothy in this way, for he saw the benefits to society resulting from Jewish beliefs and our way of life. However, he drew a line at Timothy being circumcised according to our faith. So Timothy grew up knowing about the Greek gods but having a personal faith in the one, true God of Israel. I praised God for this. My son was thoughtful and serious, emotional, timid, almost fearful at times, a quiet character but sincere, strong in his faith, a young man of integrity and purity. My mother and I delighted in him.

Timothy was just a youth when Saul and Barnabas arrived in Lystra, but old enough to understand all that went on. They came to bring us what they called the good news, teaching the Jewish belief: that there is one true God. That could have offended the Greeks if it were not for an event that took place soon after Paul and Barnabas arrived. A man known throughout the town, a man with damaged feet who had never walked, was listening as Paul preached. Paul told him to stand up and walk; he immediately did so! With that show of power, the Greeks assumed that the gods had appeared among us— Paul as Hermes and Barnabas as Zeus. The crowds and the priests from the temple of Zeus (which was just outside the town) brought sacrifices and wreaths to Paul and Barnabas at the town gates.

The two men were alarmed, assuring everyone that they were humans like us, not gods. Earnestly they spoke again of one God, the living God, Creator of all, the God who reveals himself to us through his goodness and provision for us in our daily lives, the source of joy. They urged all of us to turn to him. Then they talked of the Israelites' history and of David's descendant, the promised Saviour and long-awaited One. He had come, they said! His name was Jesus, but he had not been received by our people; instead he had been rejected in Jerusalem and crucified. But wonder of wonders, God had raised him from the dead and Jesus had appeared to many of his followers. A new relationship with God was now possible for both the people of Israel and God-fearing Gentiles. Our sins could be totally forgiven – sacrifices would no longer be necessary. Being in a right relationship with God was not dependent on anything we could do for ourselves, but by believing in Jesus.[1]

My son, my mother and I were among those who believed. We experienced joy and a very wonderful sense of community. Nonetheless, there was trouble ahead, for Jewish men arrived from Iconium and Antioch. They wanted the Jews in our town to have nothing to do with Paul and Barnabas, winning over the crowd. Timothy, alongside many of the believers, witnessed the people turning against Paul. In fear we watched as they stoned him, dragging him from the town, leaving him for dead. But we who had believed in Jesus gathered around Paul, prayed for him and miraculously he lived. I was aware that this was making an indelible impression on Timothy's sensitive and responsive nature.

We were saddened by the departure of Paul and Barnabas the next day. But how glad we were when they returned and told us that many in Derbe had believed in Christ and become disciples! Paul and Barnabas had come back to strengthen our faith with words of encouragement, appoint leaders and warn us of the hardship and persecutions faced by those who followed the Way.

Paul was to visit us again a few years later with a man named Silas. During the years between Paul's visits, I had watched Timothy grow and develop in his faith. The deep understanding of the scriptures that my mother and I had instilled within him shaped and fed his belief in Christ our Lord. Paul was so taken with Timothy's growing maturity and with his good reputation among the believers that, in spite of his young age, he asked my son to accompany him on his travels. However, he was concerned that the Jewish men whom they would meet, holding strongly to their roots, would struggle with the fact that Timothy was uncircumcised. My son, now old enough to make this decision himself, agreed to circumcision.

My pain at seeing my son's physical pain was nothing in comparison to my sorrow at parting with him. Although I took pleasure in his growing confidence, at the core of my maternal heart was a gnawing fear for his well-being. I was under no illusions concerning the possible threat to their safety. Nevertheless, I had the assurance that Timothy was walking in God's ways, the comfort of knowing that he was in God's hands and that the prophecies concerning him would be fulfilled. Paul and the church elders had laid hands on Timothy prior to their departure and he had received gifts of the Holy Spirit to strengthen and empower him.[2] I joined them in their prayers that Timothy would grow in strength, knowing the power of the Holy Spirit, experiencing and sharing God's love. We prayed that he would have confidence, self-discipline and the courage to withstand opposition, unashamed of the gospel. While my position of influence in his life was now diminishing, my prayers for him were increasing.

Over the next ten years, letters from Timothy told me of his journeys with Paul to places such as Corinth, Thessalonica, Cos, Rhodes, Philippi and Ephesus (where they stayed for two years). These letters showed a growing depth of love and friendship between my son and Paul, who went on to entrust difficult situations in churches both at Corinth and Ephesus into Timothy's care. Eventually Timothy wrote to tell me that he was with Paul in Rome, where Paul was under house arrest. After two years Paul was released and once again was free to travel and share the gospel.

Then I heard the news that I had always dreaded: my son had been imprisoned.[3] How I prayed for his release and how I rejoiced when it came! But the persecution of believers increased and Paul was imprisoned once again, this time in far harsher conditions and with little hope of release. Timothy wrote to me of the farewell letter that he had received from Paul, who had become his much-loved spiritual father. How my son must have grieved and how much he must have needed Paul's words of encouragement and instruction in order to continue the Lord's work. I have no doubt that the last decade has changed Timothy beyond all recognition and I thank God for sustaining my son. I am grateful to Paul, the man who advised and nurtured him, enabling him to become all that God intended.

Reflection and discussion

- Did any words or phrases stand out for you?

- Eunice and her mother Lois influenced Timothy's life by teaching him the scriptures and God's ways, promoting his early spiritual growth. Paul recognised the fundamental importance of their input (2 Timothy 3:14–15). Timothy went on to play a major part in the growth of the early Church and in supporting Paul. We may not be game changers but we may be in a position to care for or influence those who are. This child who had been so lovingly nurtured had the ability to love others in a genuine way. Read Philippians 2:19–22. Where do you have influence? How can you use this for good?

- Eunice needed courage to go against the prevailing Roman and Greek cultures with their belief in many gods, and to teach Timothy about the one true God, especially as her husband was a Greek. She also needed courage to live with the complexities and tensions of a mixed-race marriage. No doubt there were those who disapproved of her and Timothy because he had not been circumcised. She must have maintained a strong trust in God, understanding where she could compromise and which truths she needed to hold on to unswervingly. Is there anyone you know who lives in a complex situation and needs your prayers? There are situations both in our society and in our personal lives which create tensions within us; we need both courage and wisdom to live with them. Share these if appropriate and pray for one another. Read 2 Timothy 1:13–14. What are the truths that we need to 'guard' through the power of the Holy Spirit?

- In Acts 14:15–17, we read that Paul started teaching at the place where his listeners were in their spiritual understanding. He explained that the evidence for God's existence and goodness was all around them, demonstrated in the way God provided for their daily needs. How can we learn to explain our faith in a way that is accessible to others? You may like to read Paul's explanation to the Israelites and God-fearing Gentiles in Acts 13:16–43 in your own time.

- What evidence for God's existence and goodness do you see around you? It is interesting to note the evidence that Paul gave to the people in Lystra: 'He gives you food and joyful hearts' (Acts 14:17). How is joy 'evidence' of God's existence and his goodness? In the monologue, Eunice and the other new believers experienced joy and community. What gives joy to your heart? Read Jeremiah 15:16. What creates community in our churches and fellowship groups? Read Philippians 2:2 and 1 Peter 3:8. What insights do these verses give you?

- Eunice became part of a thriving church in Lystra. When Paul and Barnabas returned there, it had grown to such an extent that it needed a leadership structure (Acts 14:23). However, it must have also had its struggles, for we read that this group of new believers needed encouragement: 'they strengthened the believers. They encouraged them to continue in the faith, reminding them that we must suffer many hardships to enter the Kingdom of God' (Acts 14:22). Have you suffered in small or large ways because of your faith? If you are able, share these, and seek ways to encourage each other.

- Reread Eunice's description of Timothy in the monologue. She would have known and understood more than anybody his sensitive nature, and no doubt was aware how this would impact on his leadership both positively and negatively. Although Paul had such a different personality to Timothy, he saw the potential in him and grew to appreciate his sensitivity (2 Timothy 1:4), love, loyalty (Philippians 2:19–22) and quiet strength of character. All characters and personalities can be used by God in spite of our flaws and weaknesses. Be encouraged: there are many types of leaders and ways to lead. How can we live and work better alongside those who are very different to us? Pray for spiritual eyes to see the potential in others before they have matured, particularly young people and those who are young in their faith.

- Circumcision was one of the many issues that the early Church had to consider in the light of the new covenant. While circumcision was no longer necessary, respecting the traditions, heritage and beliefs of others was important when relating the good news to them. How do traditions help or hinder our spiritual growth? How can they give us opportunities to share our faith? What examples can you think of from your experiences? Are there convictions or viewpoints that you once thought were very important in Christian living that you now hold on to more lightly or not at all? How has this been liberating? Read Galatians 5:1.

- There are many examples of mentoring in the Bible and two appear in these narratives and letters: Eunice and Lois mentored Timothy. You may be able to think of other examples, such as Moses and Joshua (Deuteronomy 31:7–8) or Elijah and Elisha (1 Kings 19:19–21). Eunice's and Lois' mentoring of Timothy throughout his childhood took time and understanding. They prepared the way for Paul's mentoring of Timothy. Paul encouraged Timothy's gifting: 'Fan into flames the spiritual gift

God gave you' (2 Timothy 1:6). He exhorted and challenged him to overcome his weaknesses, and to pursue righteous living, faithfulness, love and peace (2 Timothy 2:22). He advised Timothy not to be easily intimidated by others (2 Timothy 1:8; 2:1; 4:2) or to let people look down on him because of his youth (1 Timothy 4:12). Are you in a position to mentor younger people or new Christians either formally or informally? Perhaps you feel that you would benefit from being mentored. Share your thoughts.

- Paul wrote to Timothy, 'God has not given us a spirit of fear and timidity, but of power, love, and self-discipline' (2 Timothy 1:7). Why is self-discipline so important in the lives of those who sincerely wish to follow Christ? Are there spiritual disciplines that you practice or would like to practice? How could you find out more? Share your experiences with each other.

- Timothy's ministry in Corinth (1 Corinthians 4:17) was not easy and could perhaps be regarded as ineffectual in that the church continued to have so many major difficulties; but this was not the end for Timothy. There was further ministry for him in Ephesus (1 Timothy 1:3–5). Timothy was instructed by Paul to stop both false teaching and time wasting in unprofitable conversation and speculation within the church fellowship. He was to focus on teaching, which would help the believers to develop lives of sincere faith in God. This would lead to them being filled with God's love, having pure hearts and clear consciences (1 Timothy 1:5). How can we develop such lives? Have there been times when you have felt unsuccessful or disappointed in a ministry? If you are able, share this. Take encouragement from the life of Timothy— the Lord has more in store for you, as he did for Timothy.

- Eunice would have found it hard to hear of her son's struggles in ministry, and his imprisonment must have distressed her. In many ways, it is harder to see those we love struggling with disappointment and adversity than it is to manage our own setbacks. There may be those you love who are going through particular difficulties at the moment and who you would like the group to pray for. If you are able, take this opportunity.

- Eunice passed on the baton of spiritually supporting her son to Paul. In his letter (2 Timothy), Paul, aware that his death was near, passed on the leadership baton to Timothy. This letter is packed with advice for him, and us. Do you need to trust a younger person with responsibility or relinquish a task to somebody else? Perhaps it is time for you to take the baton from somebody else. Share your thoughts.

- Eunice was no longer in a position to directly advise her son, but no doubt supported him lovingly in prayer and was grateful to Paul for giving him relevant knowledge, expertise and fatherly affection. Share times when you have observed others giving your loved ones the support they needed. Thank God that we are part of his family and for his provision for our needs.

Conclusion

Take time to pray through your findings. What might God be saying to you? Is anything particularly relevant to your life at the moment? Write down what you have learnt and refer back to it regularly in the days ahead so that it becomes part of your thinking, reacting and lifestyle.

Notes

Hagar (2)
1 Genesis 17
2 Genesis 18:1–16

Shiphrah, Puah and Jochebed
1 Exodus 1:16
2 Genesis 38:28–30
3 Genesis 47:27
4 Genesis 15:14, NIV
5 Exodus 1:16
6 Genesis 17:1
7 Genesis 16:13
8 Genesis 21:33
9 Genesis 22:14

Deborah
1 Judges 5:2
2 Judges 5:31

Jael
1 Exodus 20:13
2 Leviticus 19:18

Jephthah's daughter
1 Leviticus 18:21

Michal (1)
1 1 Samuel 15:22–31
2 1 Samuel 16:14–23
3 1 Samuel 19:1–3

Michal (2)
1 1 Samuel 31:1–13
2 2 Samuel 1:23–26
3 2 Samuel 3:1–5
4 2 Samuel 5:6–7
5 2 Samuel 5:13–16

6 2 Samuel 6:1–12
7 1 Samuel 13:14

Abigail (2)
1 1 Samuel 26
2 1 Samuel 27:8–12; 29:1–11
3 1 Samuel 29
4 2 Samuel 1
5 2 Samuel 1:26, ESV
6 2 Samuel 2:10
7 2 Samuel 3:1
8 2 Samuel 4
9 2 Samuel 5:1–5
10 2 Samuel 5:9,13

The queen of Sheba
1 1 Kings 4:29–34
2 1 Kings 4:20–21
3 1 Kings 7:1–12
4 1 Kings 4:34
5 Ecclesiastes 1:9
6 Ecclesiastes 1:11
7 Ecclesiastes 1:8
8 Ecclesiastes 3:11
9 Ecclesiastes 2:26
10 Ecclesiastes 3:1–2
11 Ecclesiastes 12:13–14
12 Proverbs 20:9, ESV
13 Ecclesiastes 12:1

The woman from Shunem (1)
1 Proverbs 31:10–31
2 1 Kings 18:16–39

The young Jewish maid
1 2 Samuel 8:5–6
2 1 Samuel 16:7

Tabitha or Dorcas

1   Acts 9:2
2   Acts 7:54–60; 8:1
3   Acts 6:5
4   Acts 8:40
5   Isaiah 53:7–8
6   Acts 8:26–40
7   Philippians 4:7
8   Matthew 25:40
9   Acts 6:3
10 Acts 9:32–35
11 Acts 3:1–10

Mary of Jerusalem

1   Acts 8:3
2   Psalm 84:5–8
3   Colossians 4:10
4   Acts 9:26–27
5   Acts 4:36
6   Acts 4:36–37
7   Acts 5:17–20
8   Mark's Gospel
9   1 Peter 5:13
10 Acts 13:5
11 Acts 13:13
12 Acts 15:1–31
13 Acts 15:36–41
14 Colossians 4:10; Philemon 24;
    2 Timothy 4:11

Lydia

1   Psalm 42:1
2   Acts 16:9–10
3   John 14:15–17
4   John 19:2, 19
5   Acts 10:1–2
6   Philippians 4:10–19

Priscilla

1   Acts 9:1–31
2   2 Corinthians 11:8–9
3   Mark 1:4–5
4   Matthew 28:18–20
5   Luke 3:16
6   Romans 6:3–4, ESV
7   Galatians 3:27
8   2 Corinthians 3:16–17
9   Galatians 5:1
10 1 Corinthians 3:3–9
11 2 Timothy 4:19

Phoebe

1   Acts 18:1–5
2   Acts 18:11
3   Acts 18:18
4   Numbers 6:18 (See also Acts
    21:20–24)
5   Acts 20:2–3
6   Acts 19:21
7   Romans 3:23
8   Romans 6:23
9   Romans 5:8
10 Romans 8:1
11 Romans 10:9–10
12 Romans 8:14–17; 12:4–8
13 Acts 27–28
14 Acts 20:3–4

Eunice

1   Acts 13:38–39, taken from
    Paul's teaching in the
    synagogue at Antioch of
    Pisidia
2   1 Timothy 1:18; 4:14
3   Hebrews 13:23

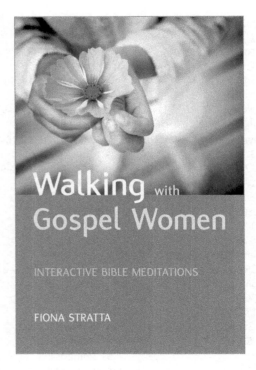

Imaginative meditation can be a powerful way of attuning ourselves to God's presence, involving as it does the emotions as well as the mind. This book offers a refreshing and inspiring way into Bible study, using meditative monologues based around many of the women of the Gospels. Through a time of guided reflection, we identify with the woman concerned and see what lessons emerge for today as we ponder her story.

Walking with Gospel Women
Interactive Bible meditations
Fiona Stratta
978 0 85746 010 3 £7.99

brfonline.org.uk

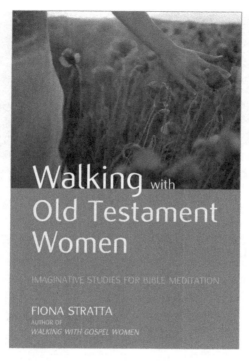

The world of the Old Testament can seem remote, yet if we take a meditative approach to reading its stories, we can find ourselves connecting the people and events of those far-off centuries with our own lives. Taking twelve women characters, some familiar, some less-known, Fiona Stratta uses monologues and reflective questions to explore what their experiences can teach us today.

Walking with Old Testament Women
Imaginative studies for Bible meditations
Fiona Stratta
978 0 84101 718 1 £7.99

brfonline.org.uk

Transforming
lives and communities

Christian growth and understanding of the Bible

Resourcing individuals, groups and leaders in churches for their own spiritual journey and for their ministry

Church outreach in the local community

Offering three programmes that churches are embracing to great effect as they seek to engage with their local communities and transform lives

Teaching Christianity in primary schools

Working with children and teachers to explore Christianity creatively and confidently

Children's and family ministry

Working with churches and families to explore Christianity creatively and bring the Bible alive

Visit **brf.org.uk** for more information on BRF's work
Review this book on Twitter using **#BRFconnect**

brf.org.uk

The Bible Reading Fellowship (BRF) is a Registered Charity (No. 233280)